Walk!

The Peak District (South)

with

Frank Westcott

DISCOVERY WALKING GUIDES LTD

Walk! The Peak District South
First Edition - January 2006
Copyright © 2006

Published by
Discovery Walking Guides Ltd
10 Tennyson Close, Northampton NN5 7HJ,
England

Mapping supplied by **Global Mapping Limited**
(www.globalmapping.com)

Mapping sourced from Ordnance Survey® This product includes mapping data licensed from **Ordnance Survey®** with the permission of the Controller of Her Majesty's Stationery Office. © Crown Copyright 2005. All rights reserved.
Licence Number 40044851

Photographs
All photographs in this book were taken by the author, *with the exception of the author pictures on Page 7 & 19, taken by Emma Westcott.

Front Cover Photographs

**Lathkill Dale & Parson's Tor
(Walks 13 & 16)**

**Pickering Tor
footbridge, Dovedale
(Walk 8)**

**Trig Point, Wolfscote
Hill (Walk 10)**

**Monsal Dale & Viaduct
(Walks 19-22)**

ISBN 1-904946-11-9
Text and photographs* © Frank Westcott

Walk!
The Peak District
(South)

CONTENTS

THE WALKS

THE AUTHOR

Following an upbringing in the Home Counties and university in Leeds, Frank Westcott's work as a Geotechnical Engineer took him across Eastern and Southern Africa for a decade, designing and supervising construction of dams, roads, bridges and water supply development projects. After his return to the UK, and a brief spell building a motorway in Scotland, he now works on cleaning up derelict and polluted 'brownfield' land for redevelopment, as a senior engineer for an environmental consultancy.

His love of upland walking was kindled in his youth during family holidays in Wales and the Lake District - he climbed Cader Idris with his father at the age of seven - and rediscovered after his return from Africa. He has lived with his family in the Peak District for the last 11 years and regards it as some of the finest walking country to be found anywhere. He also enjoys photography, a good pint and the Fray Bentos range of pies (he eats all of them). As an author his previous publications have been professional journal and conference articles on absolutely riveting subjects like monitoring groundwater pollution from rubbish tips and redeveloping contaminated land.

photo © Emma Westcott 2005

ACKNOWLEDGEMENTS

Exactly a year has passed since the first walk in this book was researched and since the start of Right to Roam in the Peak District; a good time to acknowledge those whose assistance has been crucial to this project. Thanks are due to my family; Rob for helping on some of the walks, Emma for helping with photographs and the index, and Ann for her support and forbearance during this time. The publishers and the series editors David and Ros Brawn provided the initial inspiration, critical support, feedback and on occasions censorship, for which I am grateful. Thanks also go to the many anonymous walkers and others I met on my travels, for information and advice freely given, to which I hope I have done justice in this book.

Frank Westcott
19th September 2005
westcottwalkpeakdistrict@hotmail.co.uk

I set out to choose and describe the walks in this book from a distinctive perspective. The Peak District is a beautiful landscape: but above the bedrock of the Carboniferous gritstones and limestones it is almost entirely a man-made one. From prehistoric to industrial times the people who lived here have been the prime movers in shaping the landscape.

Rock-built field barn

The ancient wild wood has been cleared, rocks picked from the thin stony soil and piled up in walls or used to build field barn and farmhouses. Stone has been quarried and burnt for lime or cut to shape for building. Minerals have been discovered and mined: copper at **Ecton** from the Bronze Age, lead since Roman times and even coal from the moors above **Buxton** since the industrial age.

Ancient packhorse trails, drove routes, turnpikes, tramways, railways and modern highways have been driven across the high plateaux and passes of the Peak. Towns and villages have grown where water was plentiful, where roads or railways met or where lead mines or stone quarries provided a livelihood.

Today's landscape

What makes walking in the south Peak District so interesting is that this is a landscape of constant change, from the annual rhythm of the farming seasons to the slower changes to land use and human activities that take place over generations. This is no 'unspoiled' landscape, but it absorbs and heals the scars of man's activities over the years, from copper and lead mining to quarrying; all have become essential components of the landscape we see today.

The potential for modern industrial-scale development to create disfigurement on a grand scale is balanced by the strict controls that come with being a National Park: but it would be a denial of history if the desire to keep the place 'unspoiled' was to bring a complete end to human activity in the Peak District, and the dynamic shaping of this landscape that this has brought about from the beginning of history.

AIM & SCOPE

These walks are aimed at 'Adventurous Leisure Walkers', who want their walking to be enjoyable, interesting and challenging. Most walks are between 10 and 20 km (6 to 13 miles) long, taking between 3 and 6 hours: but many have shorter alternatives built-in, and '20 mile masochists' can combine walks and have something to brag about in the pub afterwards.

I started the field research on the day, 19th September 2004, that 'Right to Roam' came into force in the Peak District and have taken maximum advantage of these new access rights to describe 'new' walks, both in areas previously neglected and to provide a new perspective on familiar areas such as Dovedale and the moors above Buxton.

Ninety-five percent of today's walkers will arrive and leave by car, and so most of the walks are described as circular routes. Some linear walks are included, simply because they work better that way, and these are accessible at both ends by a bus service, so motorists can park at one end, get the bus out to the other, and walk back.

All the walks (except for Walk 28) are accessible by bus, though the services may not be frequent and may run only on certain days, making a certain amount of planning necessary. The south Peak District is surprisingly accessible by bus, and a ride on an almost empty country bus can be a much more enjoyable experience than a congested crawl down the A6.

Above all, I want the walks to be interesting as well as beneficial to health and fitness, and to help the visitor come away with a better understanding and feeling for the landscape of the Peak district and the natural forces and human life that has shaped it.

THE PEAK DISTRICT SOUTH AREA

The walks in this book are all within the Peak District National Park, south of a line formed by the A537 **Cat and Fiddle** road, **Buxton**, the A623 **Tideswell Moor** road, **Baslow** and the A619 **Robin Hood** road to **Chesterfield**. The whole area is covered by the Ordnance Survey Explorer sheet OL24, which the OS, misleadingly, calls the White Peak Area, since some of the finest Gritstone (Dark Peak) country is covered by this map. The walks encompass contrasting Gritstone and Limestone country, from the moors above **Macclesfield** and the **Roaches** of Staffordshire, to the limestone dales of **Dovedale** and the **Lathkill**.

Areas outside the National Park boundary have been excluded, a hard decision, since some fine walking country lies just outside the park. To those who love these areas, and for those who long to explore parts of the northern Peak District such as **Edale**, the **Hope** and **Goyt Valleys** and the moors of **Combs Moss**, **Kinder Scout**, **Bleaklow** and the **Derwent Edges**, I ask that you have patience to await future guides.

THE LANDSCAPE

The Peak District is an upland area at the southern end of the Pennines, between the industrial cities of **Manchester**, **The Potteries**, **Sheffield** and **Derby**. It actually has very few peaks, but consists of a series of plateaux and escarpments ('Edges') cut through by deep valleys, some carrying rivers, others dry. The contrasting limestone and gritstone bedrock gives rise to two distinct landscape types.

Typically the limestone 'White Peak' landscape consists of an open plateau

criss-crossed with drystone walls (Walk 17), dissected by steep sided gorges or 'Dales', with exposed limestone crags rising above wooded slopes (Walks 4-11, 16, 21-22). Water flows in underground channels (helped by the lead miners who cut drainage tunnels or *soughs* to keep water out of the mines: Walks 1 & 18) and despite high rainfall, rivers do not flow across the surface of the plateau. Around 26,000 miles of drystone walls in the White Peak (Walk 17) have been built and maintained by generations of farmers, and

Exposed limestone crags

together with the stone barns and farmhouses, give the area its distinctive appearance.

The gritstone Dark Peak presents an altogether more rugged landscape. The alternating layers of shale and gritstone give rise to a stepped landscape, with the erosion resistant gritstone forming

Dramatic gritstone crags

escarpments or 'edges' (Walks 29-32). The land ranges from poor waterlogged grazing on the shale outcrop (Walk 7), to the moors of cotton grass and heather at higher level, with the gritstone exposed in dramatic crags (loved by rock climbers) on the scarp slopes (Walk 29). Where gritstone sits above soft shales landslipping is common, creating dramatic features such as the chasm of **Luds Church** (Walk 28).

GEOLOGY

Chrome Hill and Parkhouse Hill

The Peak District was born 325 million years ago in the lower Carboniferous period, in a lime-rich tropical sea. Volcanoes formed islands in the sea, rather like a Pacific atoll, fringed with an early form of coral reef, which created the 'reef knoll' hills fringing **Dovedale**, particularly **Chrome** and **Parkhouse** hills (Walks

26&27) and **Wetton** and **Ecton** hills (Walks 1-6). Massive blocky limestones, such as those exposed in the cliffs of **Miller's Dale** and **Chee Dale** (Walks 19-22), were laid down in deeper water.

Limestone strata are separated by basalt lava flows, called 'Toadstone' by the lead miners. These are impermeable and obstruct percolation of water through the limestone, giving rise to springs (Walk 17). Mineral veins in the limestone contain ores of lead, copper and zinc.

Current bedding

Meanwhile a mountain range of Himalayan scale had formed in what is now the Scottish Highlands. Its erosion by south flowing rivers formed large deltas in the tropical sea, washing in eroded sand and mud, covering the limestone and solidifying to form the sequences of alternate layers of gritstone and shale that we now call the Millstone Grit formation. Current bedding and ripple markings formed in the deltas can still be seen in the gritstone (Walk 29).

Later geological forces pushed these rocks up into a dome, and erosion then sliced off the top of the dome, cutting right down to the older limestones in the middle but leaving the younger Millstone Grit Formation exposed around the edges, in the form of an up-ended horseshoe. Looking east from the top of **Axe Edge** (Walk 30) we can see how this has formed the two distinctive landscapes of the 'White Peak' limestone outcrop and the 'Dark Peak' of the Millstone Grit.

The final geological influence on the landscape came during the ice ages. Permafrost prevented water infiltrating into the limestone and torrents of snowmelt water carved the deep gorges into the limestone that we now know as **Dovedale** (Walks 6-9), **Wyedale** (Walks 19-22) and **Lathkill Dale** (Walks 13, 16).

HISTORY: AGRICULTURE & INDUSTRY

Nine Ladies stone circle, Stanton Moor

People have occupied and travelled through the Peak District, and shaped its landscape, since prehistoric times. Their relics remain at sites such as **Arbor Low** (Walk 13) and **Stanton Moor** (Walk 14), in ancient trackways crossing the landscape, in the open moorlands (Walks 30-32) that resulted from the clearance of the wild wood, and in cultivation terraces marking the beginning of arable farming (Walks 5, 17).

Medieval pioneers of farming in this terrain were the monasteries, whose farmsteads, called *granges*, prospered on land gifted to them by the warlords of these times, who thought it was worthless (Walk 12). Such prosperity attracted covetous eyes. The Reformation provided the pretext for a monumental land grab of the assets of the monastic houses, with the great **Chatsworth** and **Haddon** estates (Walks 24, 25) carved out from the former monastic holdings. Many of the *grange* farmsteads on the limestone grazing land are now tenanted estate farms.

Smallholdings, Axe Edge

Away from the great estates and monastic *granges* the land was farmed by family smallholders, relying on a few fields and a share of common grazing on unenclosed moors to scratch out a meagre existence. High altitude, wet and cold climate and thin rocky soil makes agriculture a tough lifestyle in this region, and the enclosure of common grazing lands in the 18th and 19th centuries, exploited as a further land grabbing opportunity, made many farm holdings uneconomic.

Those that we see today (Walk 30) have survived only because of additional income from lead mining and lime burning, and more recently from fluorspar mining, quarrying and stone-trucking (Walks 12, 17, 23, 27).

Exploitation of the Peak District's mineral wealth has a history at least as old as farming. Ecton was mined for copper in the Bronze Age (Walk 1) and the finding of Roman lead ingots confirms the antiquity of the lead mining industry. Until the 18th century mining was carried out by family businesses in small scale mines with only horses to provide motive power (Walk 18).

Mining at Longstone Edge

Steam power led to deeper, more capital intensive mining, but economic reserves were quickly exhausted and the industry went into a prolonged decline.

The last major mine, **Millclose** near **Darley Dale**, closed in 1940 (Walk 14), although reworking of the lead veins for fluorspar and calcite, thrown away as useless *gangue* by the lead miners, still continues at **Long Rake** (Walk 17) and **Longstone Edge** (Walk 23). As lead mining declined, lime burning and quarrying expanded, following the

East Buxton Lime kiln

opening of the Cromford and High Peak Tramway (Walks 12, 27) link to the canal system, and later the main line railway network. Aided by the purity of the limestone, this industry covered the country around **Buxton**, much of it excluded from the National Park (Walks 17, 21, 22). Earlier abandoned quarries have been recolonised by nature and are now protected as nature reserves or amenity areas (Walks 21, 22, 27).

The traditional link between family farming and independent industrial employment lives on today in the stone haulage business. Most stone-trucks are owner driven, often by small farmers, and on a weekend walk you'll see them parked beside the farm tractor on these smallholdings (Walks 12, 17, 30).

A derelict farmstead

Without extra income from industrial employment, most family farm holdings would have long since disappeared and the Peak District would be an unpopulated land of vast shooting estates, prairie livestock ranches, lost villages and derelict farmsteads.

The link between agriculture and industry has been the single most important factor in creating today's unique and interesting Peak District landscape over two millennia.

It will probably not survive this generation, thanks both to the dismal economics of upland farming, and to well-meaning attempts to keep the landscape 'unspoiled' by ending industrial activity in the National Park. Farmhouses, cottages and barns may remain, but if they are only occupied at weekends or in the holidays, there will be no children at the schools, no winter customers for the pub or the newsagents, and no community life in the villages - a far greater loss to the character of the Peak District than that caused by quarries and stone trucks.

PEAK DISTRICT WALKING Right to Roam-Responsibility to Respect

The Peak District was one of the first areas where mapped areas of mountain and moorland were opened up to access as of right by the Countryside and Rights of Way Act, on 19th September 2004. This was the culmination of over a century of campaigning, in which the Peak District was the crucible, the spark lit by the 1932 Kinder Scout mass trespass: sadly, Benny Rothman, its instigator, did not live to see this day.

'Right to Roam' access land is marked by the 'marooned hiker' symbol of a lone walker on the hills. Together with National Trust and Forestry Commission access land, it is shaded yellow on the latest OS Explorer mapping. In the Peak District, as well as high gritstone moorland, many of the steep sides of limestone dales have been designated as access land. 'Right to Roam' is not an absolute right and many restrictions remain. Landowners may temporarily close access land, subject to giving notice; certain users, particularly people with dogs (Walks 30, 31), are excluded altogether from some areas. These restrictions, often enforced to protect the natural environment, should be respected: details can be found on: www.countrysideaccess.gov.uk

Whilst people have the right to pass freely across designated access areas, I have observed a problem with fences and field boundaries, which can prevent or make this access difficult. Although walkers may cross fences and field boundaries running across access land, they must not be damaged. Drystone walls should never be climbed except at stiles: negotiating fences may be possible. Where fences or field boundaries create a potential obstacle to walks in this book (for example, Walk 21) I have indicated an alternative route.

Unfortunately I have observed a number of cases where new fencing has been built across access land, without stiles being provided, after the 19th September 2004 commencement date. If this has been done with the intention of obstructing walkers it is a short sighted move: walkers and farmers need to maintain a mutual respect in the countryside. Walkers need to respect the needs of farmers to keep stock secure and unmolested by dogs, and farm buildings and equipment undamaged and left alone. At a time when upland farming faces economic challenges, farmers need the support of walkers and other urban taxpayers for their role as custodians of the landscape. Right to Roam brings a responsibility to respect.

Public 'Right of Way' signposts

PUBLIC RIGHTS OF WAY

Where land is not designated as access land the only legal right to cross it is on a public right of way or by permission of the landowner. Several varieties exist:

Public footpaths may be used by people on foot, including with dogs but only when on leads. They are marked by yellow waymark arrows .

Public bridleways may also be used by horse riders and cyclists. They are marked by blue waymark arrows.

A confusing range of **Byways** exist, sometimes marked by red waymark arrows. Some carry vehicular rights, from the days of the horse and cart, but modern vehicular users are likely to be the whoop and holler merchants in 4WDs, who churn them up, making them unpleasant and dangerous to walkers. The law may soon be changed to ban motor vehicles from byways.

The **public road network** may be used by walkers, though traffic on most A and B roads will put off many walkers. In this

Public Footpath sign

book I have described small, narrow local roads as '**lanes**' and wider highways with through traffic as 'roads'. Motor traffic on both requires care and respect.

Concessionary or **Permissive** paths are not rights of way but are used by permission of the landowner, which may be withdrawn (likely if damage is caused or if dogs worry stock). Often not shown on OS maps, they may be waymarked with white arrows. Examples are the the the path over **Chrome Hill** (Walks 26, 27) and paths through **Chatsworth** park (Walk 25).

If setting out properly prepared, these walks are not unduly hazardous, but high ground and moorlands, in particular, should be treated with respect. For those inexperienced in upland walking, gaining experience with less difficult lower level walks, before tackling the higher ground, is advised. Specific safety issues are identified for each walk described in this book. General issues to be aware of are:

Weather!

- **Traffic**: care needed on roads and lanes, and crossing main roads. Walk on the right, facing oncoming traffic.

- **Weather:** Check the weather forecast, anticipate the worst case scenario. Appropriate weatherproof clothing/footwear should be worn or carried. High moorlands carry risks of exposure, hypothermia. Avoid the high moorland walks in low cloud, hill fog, falling snow or thunderstorms.

- **Injury:** from inappropriate footwear or slippery conditions, particularly well worn limestone. Take care near top or bottom of crags.

Old mineworkings

- **Lone walking:** less hazardous in good weather, and on paths in well frequented areas. Avoid being overtaken by nightfall. Let people know where you are going and when you expect to be back.

- **Old mineworkings:** should never be entered. Shafts may not be recorded or capped.

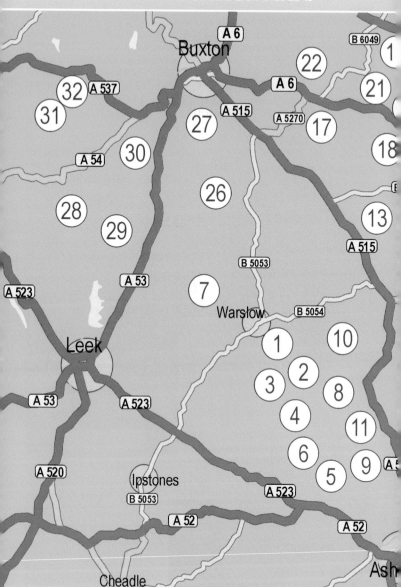

GPS RECEPTION

Sections of walks in this book with poor GPS reception are as follows:

1 Wps. 17-19	**8** Wps. 21-23	dales, mainly Wps. 1-
3 Wps. 13-15, 18-3	**9** Wps. 18-19, 22-23, in	2, 9-12, 22-23
5 Wps. 12-14	old railway cuttings	**13** Wps. 15-19
7 vicinity of Wp. 11	**10** sections in bottom of	

SYMBOLS RATING GUIDE

 our rating for effort/exertion:-
1 very easy **2** easy **3** average
4 energetic **5** strenuous

 approximate **time** to compl
a walk (compare your times
against ours early in a walk
does not include stopping ti

 approximate walking **distance** in miles/kilometres

 250m approximate **ascents/descents** in metres (N=negligib
850m

 circular route **linear** route **figure of eight** route

 risk of **vertigo**

 refreshments (may be at start or end of a route only)

- Walk descriptions include:
- timing in minutes, shown as (40M)
- compass directions, shown as (NW)
- heights in metres, shown as (1355m)
- GPS waypoints, shown as (Wp.3)

Notes on the text
Place names are shown in **bold t**
except where we refer to a wri
sign, when they are enclosed in sin
quotation marks. Local or unus
words are shown in *italics*, and
explained in the accompanying text

ORDNANCE SURVEY MAPPING

All the map sections which accompany the detailed walk descriptions in Walk! The Peak District South are reproduced under Ordnance Survey licence from the digital versions of the latest Explorer 1:25,000 scale maps. Each map section is then re-scaled to the 40,000 scale used in DWG's Walk!/Walks series of guide books. Walking Route and GPS Waypoints are then drawn onto the map section to produce the map illustrating the detailed walk description.

Walk! The Peak District South map sections are sufficient for following the detailed walk descriptions, but for planning your adventures in this region, and if you to divert from the walking routes, we strongly recommend that you purchase the latest OS Explorer maps.

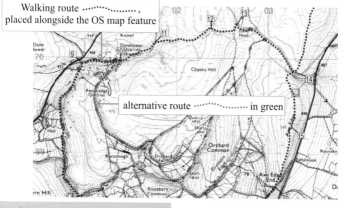

Walking route ....,
placed alongside the OS map feature

alternative route .... in green

The GPS Waypoint lists provided in this book are as recorded by Frank Westcott while researching the detailed walk descriptions. Waypoint symbols are numbered so that they can be directly identified with the walk description and waypoint list. All GPS Waypoints are subject to the accuracy of gps units in the particular location of each waypoint.

In the dramatic landscapes of the Peak District GPS reception is surprisingly good for the majority of Frank's walking routes (see pages 16-17).

Satellite Reception
Accurate location fixes for your GPS unit depend upon you receiving signals from four or more satellites. Providing you have good batteries, and that you wait until your GPS has full 'satellite acquisition' before starting out, your GPS will perform well in the Peak District. Where Frank has encountered poor satellite reception it is mentioned in the walk description.

Manually Inputting Waypoints
GPS Waypoints are quoted for the OSGB (Ordnance Survey Great Britain) datum and BNG (British National Grid) coordinates, making them identical with the OS grid coordinates of the position they refer to. To manually input the Waypoints into your GPS we suggest that you:

- switch on your GPS and select 'simulator/standby' mode.
- check that your GPS is set to the OSGB datum and BNG 'location/position format'.
- input the GPS Waypoints into a 'route' with the same number as the walking route; then when you call up the 'route' in the Peak District there will be no confusion as to which walking route it refers to.
- repeat the inputting of waypoints into routes until you have covered all the routes you plan to walk, or until you have used up the memory capacity of your GPS.
- turn off your GPS. When you turn your GPS back on it should return to its normal navigation mode.

Note that GPS Waypoints complement the routes in Walk! The Peak District South, and are not intended as an alternative to the detailed walking route descriptions.

Personal Navigator Files (PNFs) CD version 3.01
Edited versions of Frank Westcott's original GPS research tracks and waypoints are available as downloadable files on our PNFs CD, which also includes all the edited GPS tracks and waypoints for all the Walk!/Walks guide books published by DWG along with GPS Utility Special Edition software. See DWG websites for more information

www.walking.demon.co.uk & www.dwgwalking.co.uk

GPS The Easy Way (£4.99)
If you are confused by talk of GPS, but are interested in how this modern navigational aid could enhance your walking enjoyment, then simply seek out a copy of GPS The Easy Way, the UK's best selling GPS manual.

KIT - GO PREPARED

Looking for fashion advice? You've come to the wrong author! (See right)

Walking is not immune from Designer Label culture, and on busy days you could be forgiven for thinking you're on a catwalk, not a hill walk. Birkhouse Moor, one of Wainwright's Lake District fells, could be renamed 'Berghaus Moor' - and as for David B walking around the Canaries with his pair of Mallorcan Bestards… well, let's not even go there.

My philosophy of walking kit is simple:

❶ No compromise on footwear.
❷ Protect yourself from 'worst case scenario' weather: don't leave warm clothes, waterproofs, or your brain, in the car park.
❸ Wear what you find comfortable and ignore designer labels.

Given the rigours of wet conditions in the British uplands, I prefer boots with traditional leather and deep tread designs rather than the new Gore Tex. I use a pair of decade-old 'Wainwright' boots by K Shoes, resoled with Vibrams, for summer wear, and a pair of Karrimor KSB Cheviot leather boots in wet/winter conditions - together with wool outer socks and Bridgedale 'wicking' fabric inner socks.

I wear Rohan walking trousers (unfashionable colours, bought in the sale), with waterproof overtrousers and gaiters for wet weather and bog-yomping. For wet weather I use either a heavy Gore Tex coat from my motorway building days, a mid-weight seven year old Rohan micro-weave fabric anorak (again, from a sale) for general use or a lightweight 'pack a mac' for when I don't really think it will rain. In winter I wear a fleece hat: it makes me look like a Big Issue-seller, but in cold conditions 70% of body heat is lost through the head (probably rather more for us slapheads).

A standard 25 litre day rucksack carries various bits of clobber, which might include: spare T-shirt, scarf, gloves (useful even in summer for nettles), a mobile phone, maps, whistle, compass, first aid, spare batteries for GPS and camera, cereal bars, water and/or coffee, sun hat or fleece hat, sun block cream and loo roll.

I also have to confess to using a pair of telescopic walking poles, which I used to think were the ultimate poseur's accessory on the fells: but I am now a convert, having found them useful both in slippery conditions and to reduce strain on legs and knees - as well as slashing at nettles and chasing off over-inquisitive livestock! The reason I have two? They were 'Buy one get one free' in a Mountain Warehouse sale.

1 THE MINES OF ECTON

Ecton Hill contained rich veins of copper as a result of strong folding and mineralisation of the rocks during volcanic periods around 300 million years ago. They have been mined since the Bronze Age but the heyday of the mines was in the late 18th century, when the Duke of Devonshire made so much money from them that he was able to build the Georgian Crescent and Opera House in **Buxton** and remodel **Chatsworth Park**. Few people made much money after that as the mines went into decline, with a trail of bankrupt companies, out of pocket investors and more than a whiff of fraud characterising the following 150 years. As for the miners, they worked half naked by the light of tallow candles for wages of as little as 2d (less than 1p) an hour, including children as young as five: boys in the mine, girls breaking up the ore on the dressing floors.

The mines finally closed in 1889, but nobody told the Luftwaffe, who in 1942 tried to bomb them. They missed, anyway, and blew up an empty field near **Wetton** instead, but that didn't stop the Nazi propagandist Lord Haw-Haw claiming the mission a great success.

The passage of time has removed many of the surface features of the mine; and the great spoil tips at **Ecton** became the trackbed of the **Leek and Manifold Light Railway** in 1904, now the **Manifold Way**. Nevertheless the mines left an indelible impression on the landscape of **Ecton Hill** which will be revealed on this route, while enjoying some of the finest countryside of the southern Peak District.

*Long version 3 hours and 8.1 miles/13 kilometres

Access by bus:
Nº442 **Buxton-Ashbourne** service (2 hourly, 7 days) to **Hulme End**.

Access by car:
B5054 (**Hartington-Warslow**) to **Hulme End**. Park in the National Park car park (Pay and Display).

Safety Advice
Do not enter any mine workings (some of the levels contain hidden underground shafts) or stray too close to the edge of shafts. Take particular care if walking with children and pets.

Alternative start/finish
Ecton; **Wetton Mill** (Long Version)

We start in the car park at **Hulme End**, facing south (Wp.1). To the left is a half timbered hut, formerly the terminus of the **Leek and Manifold Light Railway**, making **Hulme End** the St. Pancras of the Peak District. Looking at the ten or so houses that make up the metropolis, it's easy to see why this railway was possibly Britain's least successful, and closed a full 30 years before Dr. Beecher. However as the **Manifold Way** path it does give us a pleasant walking route through the **Manifold Valley**.

Heading along the old trackbed (SW) - now a tarmac path - we cross two bridges, ignoring the first stile on the left: though this path leads to Wp.3, it's very wet underfoot. Staying on the **Manifold Way**, we curve south until a footpath crosses, with a stile by a gate on the left (Wp.2 10M). Here we turn left, almost doubling back to head NE towards a footpath sign on the river bank which leads us to a footbridge and across the **River Manifold** (Wp.3), emerging on a lane by **Westside Mill**. We turn right along the lane, which shortly turns west to run alongside the river. At a road junction by a cottage signposted to 'Back of Ecton' (Wp.4 20M) we head straight on beside the river, passing a drystone structure with a metal gate on the left: one of the **Ecton Mine** shafts.

Here, water was taken into the mine from an aqueduct crossing the valley (now long gone), this unusual arrangement powering an underground waterwheel that drove a pump to lift water from lower levels into the **Ecton Deep Level**, and creating an underground canal used to bring ore from the mine by boat. Two hundred metres further on at **Apes Tor**, a rock cutting (Wp.5 25M) reveals the folding and disturbance that cracked the rocks, allowing the copper ore to be deposited by mineral-rich superheated water.

Retracing our steps to Wp.4, we now head uphill past a red phone box (SE) along the **Back of Ecton** lane, which takes us up a quiet side valley past a row of miners' cottages to a fishing pond on the left, built as a reservoir to supply the ore washing process at the mine, and a channel or *launder* led around the hill to the mine, its route following a line of trees on the hillside. At the reservoir's north end (Wp.6) a drainage level or *sough* used to drain into the reservoir; once it would have been possible to walk from here to **Ecton** beneath the hill.

Following the road round to the right uphill for a short length (W) to the next corner, we ignore two public footpath signs on the right. Just past the corner (Wp.7 45M) on the right is stile with a marked concession path; we pass through it and head diagonally left (SSW) up the steep side of the hill until an old spoil tip of comes into view.

This was **Bag Mine** (Wp.8), and we pass west (uphill) of the spoil tip through an open gateway. We head due (S) towards another spoil tip at **Waterbank Mine** (Wp.9 60M), its surface workings relatively well preserved. The remains of the headworks, the shafts, the ore dressing and washing areas and the spoil tips, are all visible; a good location for

Waterbank Mine

fossicking for minerals.

The trig point at Ecton Hill

Here we change direction, heading towards the trig point at the top of **Ecton Hill** (NW), following another concession path. Several old mines are dotted around, each with its spoil tip: from east to west, **Platt**, **Goodhope**, **Gregory**, **Bowler** and **Clay** mines. After a few minutes pleasant walking we reach the trig point (Wp.10 70M), admiring the views in all directions before heading down a steep slope (NE) that shortly brings us onto another track by the fenced-off mine workings of **Clayton Mine** (Wp.11), one of the two main mines of **Ecton Hill**. We turn left to head along an old miners' track (NNW), and see shortly on the left a small opening on the hillside, the remnants of a flue built to improve mine ventilation.

The track reaches a small wicket gate which we pass through to head down the hill towards the **Engine House Barn** on the crest of the ridge, passing several uncapped and poorly fenced shafts. The barn with its asymmetrical roof and several blocked up arched openings, now a humble field barn, originally housed a large beam engine that pumped water from the base of the **Ecton Mine** over 1500 feet below.

We turn sharp left at the stone wall by the barn (Wp.12 75M) (due to the deep shafts we resist the temptation to explore the barn) and head along a track that runs diagonally down the slope (SSW) between an elder tree on the left and a row of Scots pines on the right. Shortly we find the entrance to **Dutchman Level** on the left (Wp.13), one of the last to remain open, with underground workings stretching all the way back to **Waterbank**, its spoil tips providing more opportunity for fossicking. Continuing past the second row of Scots pines, we then leave the track and descend more steeply (SW) towards the top of an old quarry face.

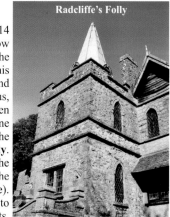
Radcliffe's Folly

We meet another well-worn path (Wp.14 85M) where we turn sharp right to follow it north towards the building on the hillside with a green copper spire. This takes us into the corner of the field, and ignoring the footpath sign in front of us, we cross the stone stile on our left, then pass under the arch connecting two stone buildings and come out in front of the building with the spire, **Radcliffe's Folly**. Built in 1931, it has nothing to do with the mines (though it is built over one of the main levels that led into **Ecton Mine**). Now sadly becoming derelict, it's easy to imagine it being inhabited by ghosts, given its atmospheric architecture!

We continue down the track until we meet a lane at the bottom (Wp.15 90M) where we turn sharp left (SE) to head past the former mine manager's house and office on our left. Shortly after passing a quarry on the left, the lane turns to head west and we pass the arched, gated opening to **Clayton Level** on the left (Wp.16), the main drainage level for **Clayton Mine**. The **Ecton Deep Level** which drained **Ecton Mine** comes out on private land by the river below the stone quarry. We continue along the road past **Birches Level**, in the trees to the left, and follow the lane around the hill until we reach a gated lane on the left with two 'No buses' signs (Wp.17 105M), where we have a choice of continuing on the main walk, or a longer alternative (see box).

For the main walk

We continue across **Ecton Bridge**. The small field to the left, **Stamps Yard**, once contained ore crushing and processing equipment when the mines were working, though all traces are long gone. After crossing the bridge we turn right onto a small footpath, following this across a small footbridge and to a stile crossing the fence on the west, after which we climb up a small bank to reach the **Manifold Way** (Wp.18) at the former **Butterton Station** (if the path is flooded, you can get here by staying on the road and turning right after 100 m, then right again by **Swainsley Tunnel**).

> **A longer alternative**
> Turning left at Wp.17 and going through the gate, and taking this lane south for around 2km, takes us through the attractive and quiet valley to **Dale Farm**, where we turn right and come to the **Wetton Mill Tea Rooms** by a stone bridge over the **River Manifold**. After refreshments we cross the bridge and turn right along the **Manifold Way**, here a motor road, and head north through **Swainsley Tunnel** to arrive at Wp.18 (Additional 60 minutes, ascent/descent 40 metres).

Heading north along the **Manifold Way**, we follow it for 1km through an attractive glade until we cross the **River Manifold** again and return to **Ecton**, where we meet a lane (Wp.19 125M). We could remain on the **Manifold Way** to return to **Hulme End**; instead we turn left along the lane and cross the bridge, following the lane (NW) as it climbs out of the valley until we reach a footpath sign on the right (Wp.20). We follow the footpath (SE) into the field but where it turns in a more easterly direction, we remain on our heading and come into the surface workings of **Dale Mine**. Unlike the mines on **Ecton Hill**, this mine was sunk for lead and its workings extended beneath the village of **Warslow**. We enjoy good views of **Ecton Hill** and you can trace the mineral veins across the face of the hill by the lines of surface workings.

Leaving the old workings, we head uphill (NE), regaining the footpath which we follow alongside the fence, then across a stile (Wp.21), and down into the valley through a pleasant, partly wooded glade. Just before we reach the **Manifold Way** we cross an old channel, the old *launder* that led water to the **Apes Tor** aqueduct. On reaching the footpath sign we zigzag to the right to find a stile bringing us back to the **Manifold Way**. We are back at Wp.2, and after turning left (N) a short walk brings us back to the car park at **Hulme End** (Wp.1 140M) where refreshments can be had at **The Manifold Inn**, on the **Hartington Road**, or bought from the village stores.

It's difficult to believe on a December morning, with the wind whistling over the hilltops and a hint of snow in the air, that 325 million years ago in the Carboniferous era, the area around **Wetton** was a tropical paradise; a Tahiti-like atoll, fringed with reefs (no palm trees though - they hadn't got round to evolving), formed from coral-like Crinoids. These consisted of a segmental stem with several segmental branches often seen as fossils in Peak District limestone. 325 million years of geology buried the reefs under younger rocks, then eroded these away; finally, during the Ice Ages, ice caps ground away softer rocks surrounding the reefs, and torrents of meltwater carved out the gorges and caves of **Dovedale** and the **Manifold Valley**, leaving the fossil reefs exposed as the steep sided hills that we see today. Some unkind souls may consider that, climatically, 'Wet 'un' (as Staffordshire folk call it) had the worst of the bargain!

The open pastures of these hills provides fine walking country, much now designated as access land by the Right to Roam legislation. Both this route and Walk 3, starting and finishing in **Wetton**, take advantage of these newly enacted rights.

This relatively short but quite arduous hike follows the tops of **Wetton Hills** and **Narrowdale Hill** on a new route, taking in the dramatic **Thor's Cave** and a short length of the **Manifold Valley**. There's also the option to pass through the neighbouring village of **Alstonefield**, considered by some to be the perfect Peak District village, its manicured verges and village greens having won it many 'best kept village' titles.

A little too chocolate-box perfect, perhaps; **Wetton**, by contrast, is a straightforward working village, with busy farmyards cheek by jowl with village houses, the church and **Ye Olde Royal Oak** pub. Rivalry between the villages goes back at least half a millennium, triggered by disputes over cattle watering rights at **Hope Marsh**, midway between the two villages.

5 | 3½ H | 6.9 miles/11km | 480m / 480m | 1

Safety Advice: (1) Limestone rock is slippery when wet, particularly in **Thor's Cave**. (2) Don't attempt in hill fog. (3) Vertical cliffs above/below **Thor's Cave** - risk of vertigo; take care and stay on paths.

Alternative start/finish
Alstonefield; Wetton Mill.

Access by bus: N°441/443 **Ashbourne-Wetton-Alstonefield-Hartington** service (limited service, Thurs and Sat only) to **Wetton** or **Alstonefield**. Nearest daily bus service is N°442 **Ashbourne-Buxton**: alight at **Alsop** old station on A515, walk to **Alstonefield** (1.9 miles/3 km).

Short version
Return to **Wetton** from Wp.15 (5 miles/8 km, 2½ hours, ascents and descents 350m).

Access by car: A515 (**Ashbourne-Buxton**) to **Milldale** turn or B5054 (**Hartington-Warslow**) to **Hulme End**, then unclassified roads to **Wetton**. Park in the free car park by the public toilets (Wp.2). Bus users start from **Ye Olde Royal Oak (**Wp.1), walk down the wide village street past some converted barns and take the first right turn, signposted for the car park, reached shortly on the right. If arriving by car, start at the car park by the public toilets (Wp.2).

From the car park (Wp.2) we head SW away from the village along a lane, turning right after around 50 metres at a junction to continue past a large dairy farm (left) and a cottage (right), to reach another junction (Wp.3 8M). Turning left (ignoring the footpath sign pointing through the farmhouse garden) we take a track on the left between two stone walls, signed 'concessionary path to Thor's Cave'; the cave and its distinctive tor come into view.

Soon after crossing a stile beside a gate, we leave the track and cross another stile on the right, signposted for 'Thor's Cave'. The path descends (W) through a dip, very muddy in wet weather, reaching a wicket gate in a fence on the far side (Wp.4). Two paths diverge here; firstly we take the path on the left, steeply uphill to the top of the tor (Wp.5 30M), being careful not to overshoot as there's a sheer drop on the other side. Just below us to the north is **Elderbush Cave** where prehistoric remains have been found, and distant views extend in all directions: a good picnic site in summer.

Returning to the wicket gate at Wp.4 we take the other path NW, descending gradually on a terrace around the hill, bringing us shortly to the entrance to **Thor's Cave** (Wp.6), which can be explored with care (slippery underfoot, a torch needed). Its name (the Norse God of War) might reflect Viking influence, or perhaps it was christened more recently by someone overcome with the Wagnerian qualities of the setting. Given its commanding location over the **Manifold Valley**, it's no surprise that this cave was inhabited by Bronze Age folk. They may have been miners: Bronze Age mining implements have been found in the **Ecton Mines** a few miles north.

Leaving the cave, we take the stepped path leading NE down into the **Manifold Valley**, keeping strictly to the path (note the many Crinoid fossils in the rock steps) until we meet a path coming in from the right (Wp.7). We turn left and complete the descent into the valley, crossing a footbidge over the usually dry bed of the **River Manifold** (in dry conditions it flows underground from **Wetton Mill** to **Ilam**) and reaching the **Manifold Way** (Wp.8 50M).

Turning right, we follow the tarmac cycle/footway for 800 metres alongside the **River Manifold** to a lane at a gate, just past a bridge (Wp.9 60M) which we cross, going through a small car parking area opposite. Over a stile by a 'National Trust' sign into access land, we follow a green track due N along a dry valley (frequented by birdlife including the rare Green Woodpecker).

Where the valley makes a sharp turn to the right, a footpath sign (Wp.10) indicates a path left; this optional diversion takes us to the tea rooms at **Wetton Mill** by following the path through a gate over the low ridge, where it turns sharp right to descend to **Wetton Mill** (Wp.11): note the distinctive caves in **Nan Tor** above the tea rooms. We retrace our steps to Wp.10 (75M).

From Wp.10 we go straight up the shoulder of the hill opposite on a puff and grunt ascent, heading due E, initially towards a small fenced enclosure high on the hillside. As we approach we can see the higher ground in a more ESE direction and make for this, passing S of the fenced enclosure, ultimately reaching the top of the high ground at **Far Hill** (Wp.12 90M). Taking a moment to admire the views towards the **Staffordshire Moors** and the church spires of **Grindon** and **Butterton** (oh, all right, to have a breather) we then continue to the top of the next hill to the NE, the west summit of **Wetton Hills**, keeping to the high ground on excellent open grassland walking (Wp.13 100M).

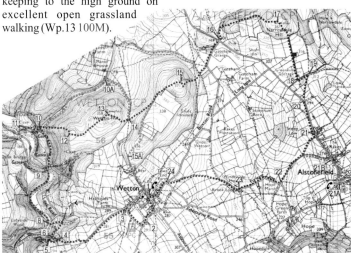

We descend E into a dip in the hills with an enclosed field, heading left (NE) to reach a stone stile where the wall meets a fence (Wp.14). (Alternative to link Wps.10-14: continue up the dry valley until reaching a 3 storey house (Wp.10A **The Pepper Inn** but no longer a pub), then take footpath on the right and follow it alongside a stone wall to Wp.14).

All routes end at Ye Olde Royal Oak

From Wp.14 we take a course directly towards the north summit of **Wetton Hills** on a NE heading, following whatever sheep tracks we can until we meet a stone wall, following this for a while before heading for the highest point (Wp.15 115M), a fine viewpoint, especially of the two neat farms of **Gateham** below to the east.

For the main route:
We descend the steep eastern slope, heading for a stile to the right of a small plantation; follow the ridge slightly SE, then before the ground gets rough take a natural terrace NE for a short while, before heading directly ENE for the stile by the plantation. From the stile we cross a field, reaching a lane by a corner and turning left, coming shortly to **Gateham Crossroads** (Wp.16 130M). Taking the lane opposite, we follow it to a gate, then head E up the side of the hill, turning slightly, then heading towards the right of some Scots pines visible on the horizon to a wall which we follow ENE until it turns sharply right.

Alternative return to Wetton (short version)
Start from Wp.15 by retracing your steps, then keep following the wall SW along the ridge, keeping SW until meeting a footpath (Wp.15A) which takes us off the hill, past a covered reservoir and onto a small lane into the village, continuing downhill to reach **Ye Olde Royal Oak** at 140M.

Here, we head east to the top of **Narrowdale Hill**, the last of our reef-hills (Wp.17 150M). Looking SSE we see **Alstonefield**, and a straight track in the foreground; we head for this, following it SSE past a camping barn and a farmhouse to a junction of tracks (Wp.18) where we turn left, coming shortly to a signposted footpath crossing (Wp.19 160M).

Alternative: to visit The George in Alsonefield
From Wp.20, continue along **Rake's Lane** for 400 metres past the toilets, then take a signposted right turn by the village green to find the pub on the right at Wp.21A. Retrace steps to where a track leaves the road on the left, descending (Wp.21B); follow this to rejoin main route to Wp.22.

We turn right, passing through a series of small fields to reach **Rake's Lane** (Wp.20) which we follow until just after the '30' sign for **Alstonefield**, then turn right onto a waymarked footpath (Wp.21 170M), following the footpath via a stile on the left into the dry valley, which we follow to **Furlong Lane** at Wp.22 (180M).

At Wp.22 we turn right and follow **Furlong Lane** W through **Hope Marsh**: note the springs on the right of the road, where a layer of shale forces the water to well up out of the limestone. Where the lane turns sharp left by stone buildings at Wp.23, we take the waymarked footpath on the right NW along the dry valley of **Windledale Hollow**, noting the tenacity of the ash trees growing out of the rock face on the right. Just after a large tree on the right, the path leaves the green track by a stone stile on the left and we follow it W, rising through a small valley across the fields, passing through a wicket gate, then heading for two large trees in front of farm buildings where a gateway leads us onto a junction of lanes at the edge of **Wetton** (Wp.24). We head diagonally across, taking the lane in front of the farm buildings into the village, seeking hearty refreshment at **Ye Olde Royal Oak** (Wp.1 210M).

3 WETTON HILL, SUGARLOAF & ECTON HILL

We start with some fine upland walking - some quite steep - on **Wetton Hills** and **Ecton Hill**, with views across the southern **Peak District** and the **Manifold Valley**, followed by an attractive section alongside the **River Manifold** between **Ecton** and **Wetton Mill** - and with a sting in the tail on the return to **Wetton**.

| 4 | 3½ H | 6.9 miles/11km | 450m / 450m | ↻ | 🍴 1 |

Safety Advice: Do not attempt in hill fog.

> **Alternative start/finish**
> Hulme End; Wetton Mill.

Access by bus: Nº441/443 **Ashbourne-Wetton-Alstonefield-Hartington** service (limited service, Thurs and Sat only) to **Wetton or Alstonefield**. Nearest daily bus service is Nº442 **Ashbourne-Buxton**: alight at **Hulme End** (Wp.12A), walk down **Manifold Way** to meet route at **Ecton** (Wp.12).

Access by car: A515 (**Ashbourne-Buxton**) to **Milldale** turn or B5054 (**Hartington-Warslow**) to **Hulme End**, then unclassified roads to **Wetton**. Park in the free car park by the public toilets.

We head NW from **Ye Olde Royal Oak** in **Wetton** (Wp.1) up the village street, forking right opposite the red phone box to follow the lane uphill to its end by a covered reservoir. Continuing on the same bearing on a footpath that leads us through two extremely narrow squeeze stiles (wishing we'd not eaten all the pies!), we reach access land at **Wetton Hill** (Wp.2 9M). The footpath takes us over the shoulder of the hill, then across a field in the dip between the hills to a stile in its corner. Across the stile, we turn left and cross the substantial stone stile over the wall (Wp.3 15M), then head NW uphill to the western summit of **Wetton Hills** (Wp.4 20M).

... **extremely narrow squeeze stiles** ...

From this vantage point we head directly for the ridge visible to the NW with a wall running straight up the side, on a steep descent, zigzagging where necessary to avoid rocks, then heading up the other side. We pass the corner of a fence and make for the rocky outcrop at the top of the ridge (Wp.6 45M).

Now two options are available: follow the ridge SSW down to **Wetton Mill** (Wp.16), or head NNE along the ridge until encountering a fence, at which point we descend the slope on the left (NW) to the **Sugarloaf**, a distinctive reef-knoll partly blocking the valley.

The 'Frank Westcott' stile

A fence bars our way, but on traversing left we come to a new stile (Wp.7 60M) - for which the author modestly claims some credit, having written to the National Trust to ask for its provision when the fence was built.

Crossing the stile, we take the path climbing steeply round the western side of the **Sugarloaf** to reach a stile by a gate, bending right to a squeeze stile in a wall, then running NE up the valley to meet a farm track at a wicket gate (Wp.8 78M).

We take a path on the left across a stone stile and head W towards a farm on the horizon; before reaching it the path crosses a stone stile by a cattle trough to the right and heads NW, diagonally uphill across the field to a gateway.

After looking back to **Wetton Hills** we continue on the same heading to a stile in the wall running along the rim of the valley, with **Swainsley Hall** directly below (Wp.9 90M). We don't pass through this stile, but instead head to the right (NE) towards two trees on the horizon, to the left of which is a metal gate through which we pass onto the open land of **Ecton Hill**. We follow the crest of the ridge over the old workings and capped shaft of **Goodhope Mine** to the trig point of **Ecton Hill** (Wp.10 98M), enjoying views across to **Warslow**, **Hulme End** and **Hartington**, with the gritstone country behind to the north-west.

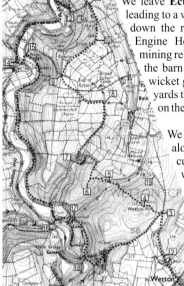

We leave **Ecton Hill** by the well used path (N) leading to a wicket gate, from where the path runs down the ridge past several old shafts to the Engine House barn (Walk 1 describes the mining relics of the **Ecton** area). To the right of the barn (Wp.11 105M), we pass through a wicket gate, follow the wall down for a few yards then pass through another wicket gate on the left.

We follow the old grassy miners' track alongside the wall down the hill, curving gently left and entering a small wood, to arrive at a rough lane by **Radcliffe's Folly** (Wp.12 115M). which takes us downhill to meet another lane where we head diagonally across to the lane leading towards **Warslow**, and turn left to join the **Manifold Way** cycle track (Wp.13 120M).

Crossing the River Manifold

The cycle track takes us along the valley along the old **Leek and Manifold Railway** trackbed, passing through a small car park to reach the portal of the **Swainsley Tunnel** (Wp.14 130M), its proportions substantial for a narrow gauge railway; standard gauge goods wagons were carried piggy back on the narrow gauge trains, which must have been incredibly unstable on the sharp corners!

In front of the portal we turn left and left again to cross the **River Manifold**. Just past the bridge we take a gated lane on the right with a 'No buses' sign (Wp.15 133M), following it for 2 kilometres through the pastoral landscape of the **Manifold Valley**, noting the **Swainsley** mine adit on the left, the old hydraulic ram that supplied water to **Swainsley Hall** on the opposite bank of the river, the round turreted dovecote, and the hall itself.

The lane bends to the right at **Dale Farm** and brings us to the old bridge and tea rooms at **Wetton Mill** below **Nan Tor** cave; a pleasant place for refreshments (Wp.16 160M).

Suitably refreshed, we stay on the eastern side of the river and take the footpath that passes through the buildings at **Wetton Mill** and heads E up the hillside behind: the reward for this fairly steep ascent is the view down the valley to **Thor's Cave**, and the chance to make a detour to inspect **Nan Tor** cave. At the top of the ridge the path turns left through a right angle to descend through a gate into a side valley (Wp.17 167M). Turning right, we walk down this quiet valley to come to a stile by a gate (Wp.18 175M).

The next section is the sting in the tail: for those to whom this don't appeal, the lane in front of us leads up the hill into **Wetton**, or we can rejoin the **Manifold Trail** and follow Walk 2a in reverse to return via **Thor's Cave**. Our route does not pass through the stile but follows the wall on the left, then turns left alongside a fence and heads NE up a ravine.

This is a steep scramble on sheep tracks, becoming rougher and steeper, and at one point somewhat overgrown, as we ascend: but eventually after a steep rocky section we come onto grassland and continue with a wall on our right, past some barns and alongside a field, until we come to the sturdily constructed stone stile at Wp.3 (205M).

We retrace our steps into **Wetton**, admiring the views over the fields towards the **Manifold Valley**. At the junction of lanes opposite the red phone box (Wp.20 213M) a short detour right brings us past the village hall to a path through the churchyard. The church bells may well be ringing; recently restored, the church tower now has a peal of six bells, one made in each of the last six centuries, from the 16th to 21st. The path emerges from the churchyard by **Ye Olde Royal Oak** at the end of our walk (Wp.1 220M).

4 THE HIDDEN DALE: WETTON, CASTERN & THROWLEY

The upper part of the **Manifold Valley** between **Hulme End** and **Beeston Tor** is easily accessible using the **Manifold Way** cycle track, but the old railway track follows the **Hamps Valley** from **Beeston Tor** to **Waterhouses**, leaving the lower valley between **Beeston Tor** and **Ilam** mostly inaccessible to walkers with only distant views possible from the rim of the dale. Our loss is nature's gain, however: most of this part of the valley carries Site of Special Scientific Interest designation, its isolation making it a haven for wildlife. The **River Manifold** between **Wetton Mill** and **Ilam** has a habit of disappearing altogether in summer, leaving a dried up river bed as it flows underground through an unexplored network of caves from a swallowhole or *shack* near **Wetton Mill** to a spring in the grounds of **Ilam Hall**; only when the cave system is full will water flow in the river.

The rivers **Dove** and **Manifold** rise within a mile of each other on **Axe Edge**, flowing roughly parallel before meeting near **Ilam**, yet their dales have remarkably different characters. **Dovedale**'s dramatic scenery of limestone cliffs, tors and pinnacles is full-on, striking, brash, exhibitionist, whilst the **Manifold**'s landscape of interlocking ridges, wooded slopes, silent riverside meadows and often-dry riverbed is quieter, gentler, more subtle and a little secretive.

This walk, and Walk 5, cover the lower **Manifold** from **Ilam** to **Beeston Tor**, coming together at **Rushley Bridge** and can be combined into a single long walk (16¼ miles/26km) or sections can be combined in various permutations. Also see the linear Walk 6 from **Thorpe** to **Hulme End**.

Safety Advice: Some old mine shafts near **Bincliff** and **Highfields Mines** may be uncapped: take care and keep to the path.

| **Alternative start/finish** |
| **Ilam** (link by Walk 3b); **Weags Bridge** car park on **Manifold Way**. |

Short versions
(1) Reduce by 2km, 130 metre ascents/descents by omitting **Castern Wood** loop

(2) After **Castern Wood** loop return to **Wetton** from Wp.5 (2 hours, 4.4 miles/7km, ascents & descents 240 metres).

Access by bus: Nº441 Ashbourne-Wetton service (limited service, Thurs and Sat only) to **Wetton**. Nearest daily bus service, Nº442 **Ashbourne-Buxton**: alight at **Thorpe, Dog & Partridge**, connect via Walk 5.

Access by car: A515 (**Ashbourne-Buxton**) to **Milldale** turn or B5054 (**Hartington-Warslow**) to **Hulme End**, then unclassified roads to **Wetton**. Park in the free car park by the public toilets (Wp.2).

Bus users start from **Ye Olde Royal Oak** (Wp.1). Walk down the wide village street past the converted barns and take the first right turn, signposted for the car park, soon reached on the right. If arriving by car, start at the car park by the public toilets (Wp.2).

From the car park (Wp.2) we head SW away from the village along a lane, ignoring the road on the right and taking a footpath left, just past a breeze block shed (Wp.3 5M), following the wall up the field before angling S towards a barn on the horizon. At the field's top, after detouring right to avoid a manure heap, we cross a stone stile by the corner of a wall to our left, instead of continuing round the barn. The path descends SSE alongside a wall to cross **Larkstone Lane** at a pair of stiles (Wp.4 20M), then crosses two fields and passing through a squeeze stile and a stone stile before emerging onto more open ground with the **Manifold Valley** on our right.

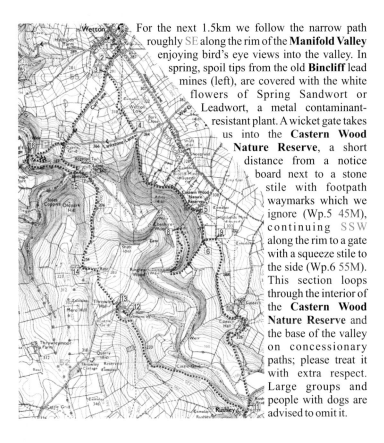

For the next 1.5km we follow the narrow path roughly SE along the rim of the **Manifold Valley** enjoying bird's eye views into the valley. In spring, spoil tips from the old **Bincliff** lead mines (left), are covered with the white flowers of Spring Sandwort or Leadwort, a metal contaminant-resistant plant. A wicket gate takes us into the **Castern Wood Nature Reserve**, a short distance from a notice board next to a stone stile with footpath waymarks which we ignore (Wp.5 45M), continuing SSW along the rim to a gate with a squeeze stile to the side (Wp.6 55M). This section loops through the interior of the **Castern Wood Nature Reserve** and the base of the valley on concessionary paths; please treat it with extra respect. Large groups and people with dogs are advised to omit it.

Ignoring the gate, we follow the wall down right on an indistinct path, passing a bench seat (a good picnic spot) and continuing with the wall on our left until reaching a wooden stile (Wp.7), still alongside the wall until the path bends sharply to the right by a signboard. Watching for birdlife, we descend steep steps past two bench seats to the riverside; now the path becomes indistinct and runs in a roughly northerly direction; stiles and waymark posts indicate our route away from stretches of the river bank reserved for wildlife.

We eventually come to the old entrance (*adit*) to **Hurts Deep Level** (Wp.8 80M) sealed with a grille gate, built to drain the **Highfields Mine**, now an important bat roost - an example of industrial history benefitting nature. Our path heads steeply up steps by a fence before turning SE and rising through an open glade, rich with primroses and orchids (don't pick!) in the spring, then climbing back to Wp.7, from where we retrace our steps to Wp.6 (100M).

Short version
Backtrack to Wp.5, pass through the squeeze stile and take the path NE across a field, passing through a squeeze stile to reach the end of **Stable Lane** which we follow NW (crossing **Larkstone Lane** and becoming **Ashbourne Lane**) back into **Wetton**.

For the main walk, from Wp.6 we pass through the stile by the gate, then follow the wall E along the head of the field to another gate (Wp.9), where we turn S and cross the field to a gate at its far side, following an ancient green trackway, then taking the lower of two tracks running alongside a wall on our right round the shoulder of the hill.

Castern Hall

Castern Hall comes into sight near a sign at a junction of paths (Wp.10 120M). We take the **Ilam** fork across a cattle grid and round the back of **Castern Hall** (tradesmen's entrance, naturally), following the track curving right past the hall (not open to the public) which becomes tarmac, and the imposing façade comes into view.

Throwley Old Hall

We keep to the tarmac lane as it wiggles down the hill, until it rounds a shoulder of the hill and becomes bounded by stone walls. Just before the walls start we take a waymarked footpath SE across fields, heading first for some trees, crossing a squeeze stile and then heading for **Rushley Bridge** where we join the lane crossing the bridge, reaching a footpath sign on the left (Wp.11 135M). (N.B. If combining this walk with Walk 5; Walks 4 and 5 meet here - also numbered Wp.11 on Walk 5.)

Continuing on Walk 4, we stay on the lane which bends sharp right (signposted 'Throwley') just before **Rushley Farm**, following it roughly NW for around 2km as it rises unfenced across an open hillside, with views across the **Manifold Valley** and across to **Castern Hall**. **Throwley** (a large farmstead behind the imposing ruin of **Throwley Old Hall**) comes into view as the road bends sharply left. We take the waymarked path on the right for **Throwley Old Hall**, close to a dewpond on the right (Wp.12). Recently conserved by English Heritage and newly open to the public, this 15th century hall exudes a spooky ambience at sunset.

We rejoin the lane at Wp.12 which shortly brings us through a gateway into the farmyard at **Throwley Hall**; the cattle barns on the left often house a range of fine bulls. When the road turns sharp left we take a footpath right, waymarked to **Beeston Tor** (Wp.13 160M). We pass left of some cattle pens, then go through a shelter belt of trees, ascending NW towards trees on the horizon and joining a farm track coming in from the right.

At the hilltop the path passes through a gateway and past a wooded copse on the left, at the end of which we follow the wall to the left (W) and descend to a footpath sign (Wp.14 170M). We turn right and head N, following the base of a dip downhill which eventually becomes a farm track to take us through two gateways and past a barn on the right, the imposing rock face of **Beeston Tor** rising in front of us, eventually following an ancient hollow way down to the riverside west of **Beeston Tor Farm**. (Wp.15 190M).

If the **River Manifold** is dry, we cross the riverbed here and take the green lane climbing the hillside opposite, meeting **Larkstone Lane** at Wp.17, a useful short-cut; if it's flowing we continue along the farm track (W), bridging the **River Hamps** (often dry as well) and passing through a camping site. The **Manifold Way** comes in from the left and runs parallel with the farm track along the south side of the river; either option brings us in 500 metres to a lane and car park (formerly **Grindon Station**) at **Weags Bridge** (Wp.16 200M).

Turning right, we cross the bridge (E) to follow **Larkstone Lane** round the hairpins (the short length of footpath on the left cuts the corner but is usually overgrown with gorse) and up hill to cross a cattle grid (Wp.17). We take a footpath on the left rising steeply NE across a field to meet **Carr Lane** at a squeeze stile, where we bear left into **Wetton**, arriving back at the car park (Wp.2 220M) and retracing our steps to **Ye Olde Royal Oak** at Wp.1 for refreshment.

5 THE GATEWAY TO DOVEDALE: THORPE & ILAM

This walk explores the villages of **Thorpe** and **Ilam**, and the hills that rise dramatically to their north, guarding the gates of Dovedale. It links with Walk 4 at **Rushley Bridge**, providing an extended walk to link with **Wetton**.

Safety Advice: (1) Treat **Thorpe Cloud** as a mountain. Wear suitable footwear and take care near cliff edges. (2) Observe any red flag warnings for the **Thorpe Rifle Range**.

Access by bus: N°442 **Ashbourne-Buxton**: 2 hourly service, 7 days, to **Thorpe, Dog & Partridge**.

Access by car: A515 (**Ashbourne-Buxton**) to **Dovedale** turn, then unclassified road to **Thorpe**. Park in the free **Narlows Lane** car park opposite the **Dog & Partridge**.

Alternative start/finish
Ilam Hall or **Dovedale** car parks (charge payable).

Short version
Omit the **Rushley River Lodge** loop beyond Wp.10 (reduce by 40 mins, 1.6 miles/2.5 km)

Note on maps: this walk obeys the First Law of Cartography (all significant detail lies at the edge of the map or on the main fold) with a vengeance!. **Thorpe Cloud** is cut by the join of the two sides of OS Explorer OL24 and the **Coldwall Bridge** section is not covered at all by this map. Trying to refold the Explorer sheet at the top of **Thorpe Cloud** in any sort of wind will either shred it or launch it across **Dovedale**!

Starting at the crossroads by the **Dog and Partridge** on the eastern edge of **Thorpe** (Wp.1), we head W past a garage along the road to **Thorpe** and **Ilam**. At the bottom of the hill by the entrance to the **Peveril of the Peak Hotel** (Wp.2), we take a footpath on the right across two small fields, to a stile by a National Trust sign (Wp.3) where we enter access land. Heeding warning signs for the rifle range, we turn left and head along the hotel's boundary fence directly towards the conical peak of **Thorpe Cloud**.

... ancient ridge and furrow cultivation ...

We cross an area formerly under ridge and furrow cultivation and pass through a gate in the wall opposite (Wp.4), then continue to the top of **Thorpe Cloud** (alternatively, head alongside the wall on the left to bring us down to the **Dove** footbridge). Much of the pastureland visible to the south shows signs of ancient ridge and furrow cultivation.

From **Thorpe Cloud** (Wp.5 20M) there are clear views of the lower end of **Dovedale** and the stepping stones to the north (check if they're submerged, if tempted to go that way!), and the surrounding hills.. (If following the more arduous alternative using Walk 8 over **Bunster Hill**, head down the north ridge towards the **Stepping Stones**.) Our route descends by the west ridge, though on reaching the erosion control fences we keep left and pick up a path that leads along a dip, descending to the footbridge (Wp.6 45M). We go left on the lane for around 100m, taking a path NW through the scrub on the right by a National Trust sign, past an access land sign and following a wall on the left, crossing the foot of **Bunster Hill**.

After passing through grassland intermixed with hawthorn scrub we reach a fence with a stile (Wp.7). Over it, we continue alongside the wall until the footpath from the **Izaak Walton Hotel** crosses, and then follow this path W to the 'nick' in the south-west ridge of **Bunster Hill** (Wp.8 70M) where we turn left to scramble up onto the ridge.

The Watts Russell Memorial

After following the ridge for around 400 metres, enjoying views of **Ilam** village and park, we bear right to descend towards the village, keeping above the bracken, then following the wall to the gate onto the road. We head W along the road into **Ilam** with the **Watts Russell Memorial on** an island in the road junction (Wp.9 90M).

The estate village of **Ilam**, built by the Watts Russells of **Ilam Hall**, is now owned by the National Trust. The architecture has a certain twee attractiveness, and you'll either love or hate the **Watts Russell Memorial**.

Turning right, we head up the village street, ignoring the main entrance to **Ilam Hall** and following the road as it curves right by the coach company's premises. Opposite the school, we take the footpath on the left following a track into the park: when it bends sharply left we continue SW, past a pond enclosed in metal railings, following a line of trees, then meeting a track coming in from the left which we follow NW as it descends to the **River Manifold** by a footbridge at Wp.10 (100M).

Crossing the footbridge, we head NW across the shoulder of the hill opposite, through a series of stiles and gateways, then descend on a waymarked route to the side of the farm at **Rushley**, reaching the lane by a footpath sign (Wp.11 115M, linking with Walk 3A). We go right, crossing **Rushley Bridge** and following the lane NE past the junction with the private road to **Castern Hall**, then going just past the isolated cottage of **River Lodge**.

We turn right through a metal gate by the front door of the lodge, noting the wooden honesty box on a pole (2 pence to pass through the lodge's grounds - bring change - this is no place to change a tenner!) and head south alongside the river to return to the footbridge at Wp.10 (140M). We continue south along the path alongside a wooded slope, now with a pasture between path and the river. On the opposite side of the river is the **Hamps Spring**, where the underground course of the **River Hamps** emerges to join the **Manifold**.

The path follows the foot of the slope as it curves SE and we reach a stile on the right, leading to a footbridge across the river (Wp.13); this would lead us via **Hinkley Wood** to **St Bertram's Bridge**, but we continue on the path alongside the wooded slope to come to the **Battle Stone** enclosed in railings, probably the shaft of an old cross. Continuing along the path by the meadow we pass through the terraced section of **Paradise Walk** (note the unusual tree by the wall on the right).

The terrace ends where the path is squeezed between rocks and river. A series of strong springs seem to boil up out of the rock - this is where the underground course of the **River Manifold** re-unites with the river bed. Ahead is the graceful arch of **St Bertram's Bridge**, our next objective (Wp.14 160M).

Ilam Hall is visible (NW); head this way to the National Trust tea room, if seeking an excellent cup of tea. Otherwise head N, following the churchyard wall. The church (Saxon or early Norman) is well worth a visit, though not in muddy boots. At the wall's end we turn right, noticing a private chapel tacked on to the church - those Watts Russells again. We follow the tarmac path back into **Ilam** village, and return to the monument (Wp.9 170M).

On the far side of the bridge over the river, we take a footpath on the left, running alongside the river across a series of flat water meadows (a pleasant amble on a summer's day), at the far end of which we pass through a stile and the path climbs over the shoulder of the hill through some scrub. This section can be muddy and slippery; it can be avoided, at the risk of a technical trespass, by taking the higher ground to the right above the scrub.

Coldwall Bridge

To the left, the confluence of the rivers **Manifold** and **Dove** is visible. Where the path crosses the hill's shoulder, signs point the way across the pastureland, through a dip and then on to a gate on a farm track leading across **Coldwall Bridge** (Wp.15 195M).

Going left through the gate, we cross the bridge, wide enough for an A road, but carrying only a farm track. A milestone reads 'Cheadle 11 miles'; once a road of importance, it is tarmacked on the north side of the bridge. Why it was

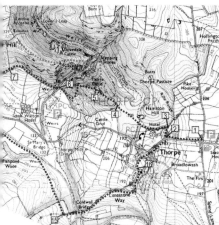

never surfaced on the south is a mystery. As it is, this is a peaceful climb out of the valley, with views over the **Dove** valley towards **Mappleton** to our right.

At the top of the hill we enter **Thorpe**, passing through a brief burst of suburbia before passing a large rectory and the smaller church, (probably Norman) on the right.

We bear right at the road junction by the old schoolhouse (Wp.16) to go downhill, where the main road comes in from the left. We continue straight ahead past the **Peveril of the Peak Hotel** (Wp.2), then retrace our steps uphill to **The Dog and Partridge** (Wp.1 210M) and refreshment.

The Dog and Partridge

Alternative route

To include the top of **Bunster Hill** (extra 100m ascent/descent): between Wp.5 (**Thorpe Cloud**) to top of **Bunster Hill** follow Walk 8. From the top of **Bunster Hill**, descend by the south-west ridge to reach Wp.8.

There are several linear walks in the **Manifold Valley** between **Thorpe** and **Hulme End** that can be done as 'Bus Out, Walk Back' routes, based on sections of Walks 5, 4, 2 and 3 and taking advantage of the 442 **Ashbourne-Buxton** bus service. Though the distance from **Thorpe** to **Hulme End** is quite long, walks can be conveniently broken for refreshments at **Ye Olde Royal Oak** at **Wetton**, and there are pubs at either end (**The Dog and Partridge** at **Thorpe** and **The Manifold Inn** at **Hulme End**) where shelter - and a pint - can be had whilst waiting for the bus.

One of the linear options is outlined here. Detailed walk descriptions and maps are as for Walk 5, Walk 4, Walk 2 Walk 3.

5 | 5H 40M | 11.9 miles/19km | 700m / 685m | 2

Safety Advice: See individual walk descriptions.

Access by bus: Nº442 **Ashbourne-Buxton** service to **Thorpe** (**Dog and Partridge**). Return on same service from **Hulme End**.

Alternative start/finish Park at **Narlow's Lane** car park, **Thorpe**, 442 bus out to **Hulme End**, walk back.

Access by car (bus out, walk back): B5054 (**Hartington-Warslow**) to **Hulme End**. Park in the **Manifold Trail** car park. Catch 442 bus out to **The Dog & Partridge** at **Thorpe**, walk back.

Swainsley Tunnel

Start at **The Dog and Partridge** at **Thorpe**. Follow Walk 5 to **Rushley Bridge** (Wp.11 115M). From **Rushley Bridge** follow Walk 4 in reverse from Wp.11 to Wp.9 to Wp.6 (omitting **Castern Wood** loop) to **Wetton**, **Ye Olde Royal Oak** (Wp.1 205M).

After refreshment, follow Walk 2 via **Thor's Cave** to **Wetton Mill** (Wp.11 275M), then Walk 3 in reverse from **Wetton Mill** (Wp.16) along the **Manifold Valley** via **Swainsley** to **Ecton** (Wp.13 320M), remaining on the **Manifold Way** to **Hulme End** car park (340M).

7 REVIDGE, & THE HIDDEN PATHS OF WARSLOW

The moderate effort required for this walk is rewarded by surprisingly good views from the hilltop of **Revidge**, and the contrast of heather moorland and grazing meadows in the countryside around, culminating in a warm welcome at **The Greyhound Inn** at **Warslow**. The top of **Revidge**, omitted from other guidebooks because no public footpath crosses its summit, is now accessible through 'Right to Roam'. Many of the footpaths on this walk suffer from under-use and can therefore be difficult to follow on the ground, but the reward is to have a tract of countryside more or less to yourself.

The landscape contrasts with the immediately preceding walks in the **Manifold Valley**, for this is part of the **Dark Peak**, underlain by shale and sandstone of the lower Millstone Grit series which gives us heather, rushes and wet grassland underfoot and warm brown sandstone in walls and buildings instead of grey limestone.

Warslow is no chocolate-box tourist village and doesn't show its best face to the road, but walk away and its true nature, a collection of smallholdings with cottages of warm local sandstone dotted around, becomes apparent. But it has been affected by the realities of 21st century rural life; two decades ago it had two schools, a police station, and a post office shop, now gone apart from one school, also under threat as pupil numbers decline. If families were encouraged to restore its derelict cottages, such services might again be viable.

2   2½ H   5.3 miles/8½km   160m 160m   2

Access by bus: N°442 **Buxton-Ashbourne** service (2 hourly, 7 days) to **The Greyhound Inn**, **Warslow**.

Alternative start/finish
Hulme End: follow Walk 1 in reverse to Wp.20, continue along the lane to **Warslow**.

Access by car: B5053 or B5054 to **Warslow**, in the village take the **Leek** road to **The Greyhound Inn**, 300 metres on right. Park in the pub car park if the landlord agrees, or carefully on the roadside without obstructing entrances.

We walk up the road (NW) from the bus stop in front of the **Greyhound Inn** in **Warslow** (Wp.1) and go through a gateway with a stone barn on our right, just before reaching **Stacey Close** on the right. Past the barn, the path goes right behind the pub, then left (NNW) through a wicket gate and across a field. A beech hedge and chain link fence forming the boundary of the **Manifold School** playing fields run alongside the path for a while; at the corner of the hedge,

The Greyhound Inn

the footpath continues ahead along an old hedge line to a wicket gate, through which our path goes slightly left (NW) across a wet area to an old stone barn by a ruined wall (Wp.2 10M). We go right (N) across a small bridge over the brook, heading north on the far side to the left of a line of trees, through a gate, past a cottage and across a combined footbridge and set of steps, then through another wicket gate. Keeping alongside a hawthorn hedge on our right, we pass **Hayes Cottage** and go through a stone stile by a gate with stone troughs beside it (Wp.3 17M).

Hayeshead Farm at Wp.4

We head diagonally uphill (NW) towards the right of two ruined cottages, arriving at a footpath sign in front of the ruined farm of **Hayeshead** (Wp.4 24M), enjoying views across the White Peak to the north and east; note the wide green track heading downhill, an old cattle drove.

The subsoil here is acidic, poor draining shale so it is understandable that these smallholder farms were abandoned, but at a time when rural housing is short and people want to live in the countryside it is hard to understand why derelict cottages such as these are prevented from being turned back into homes.

We head uphill, ignoring the first footpath sign and turning right at the second signed to 'Reapsmoor'. The official path runs along an ancient hollow way, overgrown and swampy so we stay to the right, following it as it bends uphill to a fence. We turn right, following the fence for 300 metres and crossing two stiles. When a track comes in from the right, we follow it through a gateway (Wp.5 34M) and are now on access land.

Turning due west, we take a dead reckoning west through the heather; hard going, but after only 150 metres we reach another track, and turn left (S). On reaching the Scots pines of **Revidge Wood** on the right (Wp.6 43M) we turn right onto a small path running along a low ridge above the wood and follow this until the trig point at the top of **Revidge** comes into view to the south-west. Soon afterwards the path is joined by another and this leads us to the trig point (Wp.7 50M).

Although quite an unassuming hill in its own right, **Revidge** provides excellent views in almost every direction, from **Merryton Low** on the **Morridge** ridge to the west, to the hills of **Axe Edge** and the **Cat and Fiddle** to the north-west, and round to **Longnor** and **Wheeldon Low** to the north. To the south, **Ecto**n and **Wetton Hills** and the **Manifold Valley** are spread out above the trees of **Forkhill Plantation**, rich with toadstools and mushrooms in autumn - look but don't pick as most of them are poisonous and the wacky ones are illegal as well! South of the hilltop, areas of hummocky ground reveal where **Lum Edge** sandstone was quarried for building stone. Don't be surprised to come across armed men in fatigues taking cover in these dips; army cadets train here, though no live firing takes place.

From the trig point, our path runs due west for 100 metres, then disappears. Now our route runs south-west straight across the heather, keeping to the low ridge. Occasional paths are encountered, but disappear almost immediately. A lone tree provides a landmark, and from there we head to the road by some scrub bushes, working our way round the hummocky ground.

Crossing the road with great care, we follow its verge (WNW) to a right hand bend. Just after the bend, a footpath sign by a gnarled tree on the left (Wp.8 60M) points into scrub vegetation in a WNW direction. A direct line through the scrub is impassable, but we work round to the south until **Averhill Side Farm**, almost due west, comes into view. We head in this direction, tussock-hopping across wet ground to cross a lane with two footpath signs (Wp.9 72M; to shorten the walk, turn left and follow the lane to the footpath crossing at Wp.14). On the other side we follow a ruined wall west, deviating left to cross a footbridge over a ditch, leading to a stile into a field. The path leads us through the farmyard, and we turn left just after a black fuel tank on the left hand side (Wp.10 80M) and pass into a large field.

We take a south-west course on an unclear path, heading down into a valley, **Elkstones Hill** visible opposite. We cross a fence at a stile, pass to the left of a dewpond and follow the slope downwards into a sparsely wooded area; a good picnic site. We find ourselves on a grassy glade with streams on either side, and before going too far down we step over the left hand stream and continue downhill to a wooden footbridge where shale is exposed in the stream's banks. Crossing the footbridge, we follow a fence left for a short distance at which point two more footbridges come into view (Wp.11 89M). (N.B. GPS reception is poor in this area.)

The wooden footbridge

Longer Alternative

Our route crosses the first footbridge to the left, but a longer alternative taking in **Elkstones Hill** crosses the second footbridge and follows the path into **Elkstones** (sadly, no refreshments), turning right by the telephone box. It then follows the lane uphill round a hairpin bend and take a track on the left to **Hill House Farm** from where the path zigzags up **Elkstones Hill**. The return route to Wp.11 is the same (an extra 1.5 miles/2.5 km and 40 minutes).

After crossing the first of the two footbridges at Wp.11 our main route seems to disappear; we have to climb steeply into the wood to find an indistinct path confused by many animal tracks, leading uphill and right. This steep, slippery path brings us to the head of a small ravine where the path is retained by two large timber railway sleepers.

Shortly after, we emerge from the wood into a field where a stile stands on its own, not connected to any fences, with a waymark arrow pointing us along an old hedge. We cross the hedge line to pass through a gate into another field by a small barn.

Our track heads south-east from this field, passing through a small dip with a water trough. We then follow the fence line on the left to a gateway with another track (Wp.12 112M) which we follow left, through a gate and alongside a fence. As we cross a small stream, look for a yellow arrow on a fence post (Wp.13 120M) pointing us south-west across open ground, to pass through a gateway and head for a footpath sign where the path crosses a lane (Wp.14 127M).

Our path continues east on the far side of the lane, passes in front of a barn and across a stile, then joins a green track passing through a gate, then goes between the barn and cottage of **Moorside Farm** and through another gate. Where the track curves left (Wp.15 133M) we continue on the same heading (E), crossing a stile and descending to a small valley containing a stream and a fence. After locating the stile we cross and continue up the far side (ESE), to cross a wall at an awkward, high stile with no step board. The path leads down to a hollow green track which we follow past a cottage with a dovecote. Another track joins from the right, just after which (Wp.16) we take a path through a squeeze stile to follow the field's eastern edge.

Over a narrow stile on the left where an old wall crosses the field, we cross another awkward stile onto a lane (Wp.17 140M) which we follow right, past a series of cottages and the back of the church, then reaching a T-junction by a red telephone box, noting the old enamel sign advising that telegrams may be telephoned. Sadly no longer the case - this is the old post office, now closed.

Outside the old post office

We are back at our start point opposite **The Greyhound Inn**, hopefully in time for a pint (Wp.18 150M).

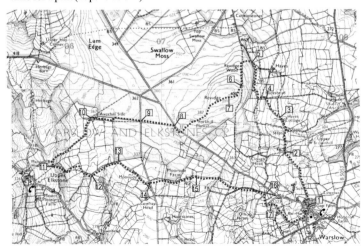

8 DOVEDALE'S WESTERN RIM

Of all the popular Peak District attractions, **Dovedale** is easily the best known and most visited. The route along the dale's base is one of Britain's most popular country walks, attracting millions of visitors every year, so you won't have it all to yourself. On a sunny Bank Holiday it can be as busy as a city pavement; even the squeeze stile by the **Stepping Stones** has a 'dual carriageway' configuration.

So, avoid it? By no means - the drama of the scenery is not diminished by the presence of others; just visit out of season or midweek to avoid the congestion. Winter is a good time, the bare trees allowing clearer views of the limestone spires and tors; spring reveals an infinite variety of greens in the young foliage, and the russets and yellows of autumn contrast pleasingly with the grey rock. Dual carriageway stiles notwithstanding, the National Trust and the Peak Park authority have done an excellent job in catering for visitor popularity without spoiling the very place they've come to enjoy.

The higher ground on the dale's sides is less visited, and though the number of footpaths providing access is limited, its ownership by the National Trust and the designation of some parts as 'Right to Roam' Access Land has opened up new walking routes in this popular area. This walk, from the **Dog and Partridge** at **Thorpe** to **Alstonefield** along **Dovedale**'s western rim, breaks new ground, and includes an ascent from the **Stepping Stones** along **Rocky Bunster** ridge to **Bunster Hill** and a route along the rim of the tributary **Hall Dale** above **Hurts Wood**, finally returning along the 'tourist path' through the dale's base. Several shorter variants are possible (see text), and the outward or return legs of the walk can be combined with the upper part of the dale between **Milldale** and **Hartington** to provide a linear walk using the **Ashbourne - Buxton** 442 bus service to connect start and finish.

Safety Advice: 1. Limestone rock is slippery when wet, particularly on **Thorpe Cloud**. 2. Take care when ascending/descending the sides of **Dovedale**; steep slopes, sheer cliffs, risk of vertigo.

Access by bus: Nº442 **Ashbourne-Buxton**: 2 hourly service, 7 days, to **The Dog and Partridge** at **Thorpe**.	**Alternative start/finish** **Dovedale** pay car park; **Milldale** (ensure car secure and belongings hidden); **Alstonefield**.
Access by car: A515 (**Ashbourne-Buxton**) to the **Dovedale** turn, then take the unclassified road to **Thorpe**. Park in the free **Narlow's Lane** car park opposite **The Dog & Partridge**.	**Short versions** Between 5.6 miles/ 9km, 2½ hours and 8 miles/13km, 4½ hours; see text.

We follow Route 5 to **Thorpe Cloud**, starting at the crossroads by the **Dog and Partridge** (Wp.1), and heading along the road (W) to **Thorpe** and **Ilam**. By the entrance to the **Peveril of the Peak Hotel** (Wp.2) we take a footpath on the right across two small fields to a stile by a National Trust sign (Wp.3 7M) where we enter access land.

Heeding the warning signs and flags for the rifle range, we turn left and head west along the hotel's boundary fence directly towards the conical peak of **Thorpe Cloud**. We cross an area formerly under ridge and furrow cultivation and pass through a gate in the wall opposite (Wp.4), then continue to the top of **Thorpe Cloud** (Wp.5 20M) from where we look north-west to **Rocky Bunster** ridge to trace the faint path that ascends the ridge from the valley floor; yes, that's where we're going next. You can also see if the **River Dove** is in flood above the stepping stones - if so, follow Route 3B down the **West Ridge** to the footbridge, then turn right along the tarmac lane to rejoin the main route. If not, descend the north ridge of **Thorpe Cloud**, following the somewhat eroded path to the foot of the dale, following the zigzags in the path as we near the bottom where **Lin Dale** on our right meets **Dove Dale** at a junction of paths (Wp.6 40M).

We cross the stepping stones and turn left past the turning circle at the head of the lane. After 70 metres, just past a small parking bay on the right (often with an ice cream van), we take a very faint path that first rises steeply up the bank to the right, then bears right, involving a slight scramble over some rocks to the top of the bluff overlooking the stepping stones.

Crossing on the stepping stones

We ascend the grassy slope (W) following a faint path where visible, keeping the woodland (and steep daleside slopes) on our right until we reach the rising crest of the **Rocky Bunster** ridge from where we enjoy excellent views in all directions (Wp.7). We follow the ridge north-west to the top, crossing the fence coming in from the left at a stile (Wp.8 80M) and on to the top of the slope (W) over another stile to reach the top of **Bunster Hill** overlooking **Ilam** (Wp.9 95M).

We follow the stone wall north, passing through a wicket gate by a 'National Trust' sign (Wp.10) to follow another wall through a field gate beside a dewpond; note its clever construction where the walls meet, so cattle in four separate fields can drink from it.

Meeting another track close to **Ilamtops Farm** (Wp.11 100M), we turn right and head east across a cattle grid towards **Air Cottage**, then follow the footpath sign on the right through a small paddock and to the slope below the cottage. The path takes a well waymarked looping course below the cottage, east then north-west past a rubbish-filled old quarry. Now the path becomes rather vague (the route on the OS map is wrong); the best course is to head up the slope towards the stone wall, then head north north-west on the farm track, pausing to admire the views over the **Dale** and **Thorpe Cloud**.

At the field's end we bear right off the track, passing through a wicket gate into beech woods (Wp.12 110M), keeping on the footpath close to the wood's edge - a most attractive section. Keep on the path - don't follow the route marked on the OS map down a precipice! - until just before the timber steps start to take the path into the valley. Here we leave the main path, cross a stile on the left and follow a wall to a gate (Wp.13 120M).

<table>
<tr><td>

Alternative route 1
Follow the path down the steps into the valley, joining the **Hall Dale** path close to **Ilam Rock**, cross the footbridge and rejoin the main route at Wp.22; 5.6 miles/9km, 3 hours.

</td><td>

At the gate we squeeze through a gap on the left, then head right around the head of a dell. We stay between the two wire fences and follow the contour round, passing through a small gate into an open area above the woods. Here we turn north-west, following sheep paths across an open area between the wall above us on the left, and **Hurts Wood** to our right, enjoying open views across **Dove Dale** and **Hall Dale**.

</td></tr>
</table>

The disused limekiln

We cross a stile in a fence into a grassy enclosure with scattered conifers (Wp.14 135M), an old quarry containing a well-preserved disused limekiln - worth a few minutes to inspect - but take care as the flue shaft at the top of the old kiln, right by the path, isn't fenced.

Lime was made by heating limestone in a wood fire to make quicklime which was hydrated to the less dangerous slaked lime, used to neutralise acid soils and improve grassland. As the raw materials of limestone and firewood were available close by, this would have been an excellent place to burn lime.

A gate with a footpath waymark at the top right hand side of the enclosure leads us onto open ground to the north with views towards **Stanshope** and **Wetton Hill**. We follow the ridge, deviating to the fence on the right for dramatic views over **Hall Dale**. At the ridge end we descend to cross a stile, then follow a steep path down to the base of **Hall Dale** (Wp.15 150M).

<table>
<tr><td>

Turning left, we follow the well-used **Hall Dale** footpath across three stiles to reach a track just before the hamlet of **Stanshope** (Wp.16)

</td><td>

Alternative route 2
Turn right and follow the footpath down **Hall Dale**, rejoining the main route at **Ilam Rock** footbridge at Wp.22, 6.9 miles/11 km, 3.5 hours.

</td></tr>
</table>

<table>
<tr><td>

Alternative Route 3
Turn right and follow the track to the top of the ridge, turning left and following the footpath down into **Milldale**, turning right at the lane at the bottom and rejoining the main route at **Polly's Cottage** at Wp.20. (8 miles/13km, 4.5 hours)

</td><td>

The main route takes us left to reach the road at **Stanshope**, with views back to **Hall Dale**. We bear right and head north along a 'no through' road which becomes a track past **Church Farm**, rich with snowdrops and daffodils in spring, continuing downhill to a lane in **Hopedale** (Wp.17 170M).

</td></tr>
</table>

We take the path opposite up the side of the dale, bearing left (N) by a lone tree to follow a wall. Where the paths cross we follow a track into **Alstonefield**, turning right at the road and following the lane past the old post office to the neatly fenced village green where we find the village pub, **The George**, on the left, for a well earned refreshment break (Wp.18 180M).

Leaving the pub, we head SE past the village green and take **Millway Lane** past the well-kept church. Just beyond the churchyard a footpath is waymarked on the right (Wp.19 185M), an alternative way to **Milldale** - a steeper descent but off tarmac. We continue along the lane (marked 'unsuitable for vehicles', but it isn't), descending into **Dovedale**, passing a small Methodist chapel and into **Milldale** hamlet whose tiny cottages once housed **Alstonefield**'s poor.

Polly's Cottage

The footpath from **Alstonefield** rejoins the road by the telephone box on the right, and at the bottom of the hill we reach a lane, the river bank left and the legendary **Polly's Cottage** right (Wp.20 200M). Teas, coffees, soup and hot pasties have been served through the stable door of this tiny establishment for nearly a century (though don't rely on it being open in midweek in winter).

Walks 8, 9 & 10 meet here, providing a range of alternative walk options.

The return leg takes us south along the base of **Dovedale**. Initially we have two options; the well-used tourist path on the river's east bank, or take the far less used path on the west bank (impassably flooded when the river is high) by following the narrow path on the right just before the public toilets: it climbs through a small wood and around the shoulder of the dale before dropping to the riverside below **Raven's Tor** joining the **Hall Dale** path to arrive at **Ilam Rock** footbridge.

The tourist path crosses the double arches of the ancient **Viator's Bridge** (named after one of Izaak Walton's 'Compleat Anglers') to follow the east side of the **River Dove** as the valley narrows by **Raven's Tor** on the opposite bank, passing the foot of the path up **Nabs Dale** and keeping straight on (Wp.21 220M; from here to **Lover's Leap** at Wp.23 the GPS will be out of signal but it's impossible to get lost).

The imposing caves of **Dove Holes** appear on our left, carved out by rushing glacial meltwater during the ice ages. The path briefly heads west before returning to its southerly course. The entrance to the narrow gorge of **Dovedale** is heralded by **Ilam Rock** footbridge (Wp.22 230M) beneath the imposing **Ilam** rock on the far bank with the tower of **Pickering Tor** beside our path. Ignoring the bridge, we continue down the dale, shortly entering the narrows where the path is supported on duckboards, soon reaching the imposing natural arch on the left, through which we can scramble to the viewpoint of **Reynard's Cave**.

Continuing south, we pass the pointed rocks of **Tissington Spires** on our left before the path rises on stone steps to the popular picnic spot of **Lover's Leap** (Wp.23 250M), the rocks of the **Twelve Apostles** on the opposite bank, only visible when the trees are leafless.

Our path descends to the river on more steps, following it to the base of **Thorpe Cloud** and passing through a 'dual carriageway' squeeze stile (Wp.24 270M).

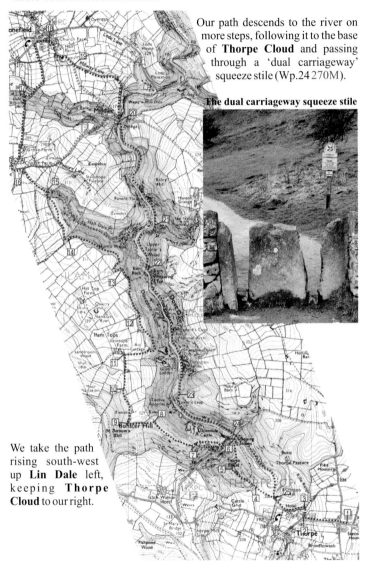

The dual carriageway squeeze stile

We take the path rising south-west up **Lin Dale** left, keeping **Thorpe Cloud** to our right.

At the top of the rise we meet our outward route (Wp.25 285M), which we retrace along the fence of the **Peveril of the Peak Hotel**, to **The Dog and Partridge Inn** (Wp.1 300M).

9 DOVEDALE'S EASTERN RIM & The Wells of Tissington

Dovedale's eastern side presents a subtly different aspect from its west when viewed from the dale's rim; less wooded, more open, a little wilder, with some splendid views of the landform and the rock formations of the dale. Although the limestone rock is over 300 million years old, the dale itself is much younger, dating from the ice ages of the past two million years, eroded by cataclysmic torrents of annual spring snowmelt runoff, when permafrost prevented water infiltrating the limestone.

There's some glorious little-known walking here, while 'Right to Roam' and the National Trust have opened up virtually the whole of the eastern rim from **Thorpe** to **Milldale** and **Shining Tor**, including the high ground to the south of **Nab's Dale** and the alligator-tail ridge of **Baley Hill**, giving us another 'new' route to explore.

We return along an attractive section of the **Tissington Trail** footpath/cycleway through the picture-postcard village of **Tissington**, an estate village originally built to house estate workers and tenant farmers. Owned by the FitzHerberts of **Tissington Hall** for the last four centuries, and famous for Whitsuntide well dressing, its quasi-feudal ambience might not please all tastes - but they must be doing something right as the multitude of thriving rural businesses (several B&Bs, a butcher, craft shop, candle maker, plant nursery, kindergarten and a tea room) would be the envy of many a struggling rural community.

As with the Western Rim walk, several shorter variants are possible, and the outward or return legs of the walk can be combined with the upper part of the dale between **Milldale** and **Hartington** to make a linear walk, using the **Ashbourne - Buxton** 442 bus service to connect the start and finish.

Safety Advice: 1. Limestone rock is slippery when wet, particularly on well used paths. 2. Obey red flag warnings for **Thorpe Rifle Range**. 3. Take care when ascending/descending the sides of **Dovedale**: steep slopes, sheer cliffs, risk of vertigo, not recommended in hill fog. 4. Particular care needed to cross the A515 at **New Inns**.

Access by bus: Nº442 **Ashbourne - Buxton**: 2 hourly service, 7 days, to **Thorpe, The Dog & Partridge**.	**Alternative start/finish** **Milldale** or **Alsop** old station (but in both cases, ensure your car is secure and belongings hidden); **Tissington** old station

Access by car: A515 (**Ashbourne - Buxton**) to **Dovedale** turn, then unclassified road to **Thorpe**. Park in the free **Narlow's Lane** car park opposite **The Dog & Partridge**.	**Short versions** See text

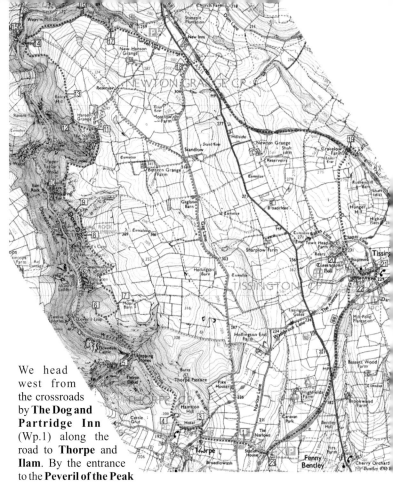

We head west from the crossroads by **The Dog and Partridge Inn** (Wp.1) along the road to **Thorpe** and **Ilam**. By the entrance to the **Peveril of the Peak Hotel** (Wp.2), we take a footpath on the right across two small fields to a stile by a National Trust sign (Wp.3 7M) where we enter access land.

Heeding warning signs and flags for the rifle range, we turn left and head west along the hotel's boundary fence, heading right (N) where it turns left past the entrance to a small quarry (Wp.4 11M). We descend (NW) along **Lin Dale** with **Thorpe Cloud** on our left, passing through a gate and reaching the bottom of **Dovedale** to pass through the **Stepping Stones** squeeze stile (Wp.5 20M). (N.B. To add **Thorpe Cloud** to this route, follow Walk 8 to here).

Lin Dale and Thorpe Cloud

Heading up the grassy bank behind the National Trust sign, we pick up a narrow path on an ascending traverse of the dale's side in a north-west direction. We follow this, occasionally looking back to admire **Thorpe Cloud** and the **Stepping Stones** and generally taking the higher option where the path forks, eventually arriving on a grassy ridge which we follow to the left until we reach a rocky headland (Wp.6 50M) with views over **Lover's Leap** viewpoint with **Twelve Apostles** rocks behind, and up the dale towards **Jacob's Ladder** rocks and the steep sided V-shaped gorge of the **Narrows**.

We round the head of the grassy valley to the north by retracing our steps along the ridge and then bear left following a stone wall, to reach a stile (Wp.7 58M) where we ignore a footpath signposted 'Tissington' crossing our route (not marked on the OS Map) to continue north-west with the stone wall on our right, to a gate with a 'concession path' waymark. Surprisingly, although the next 1½km of the daleside is National Trust owned, it isn't designated as access land, though we can use the concession path to follow the dale rim.

The wall turns sharp right two hundred metres past the gate, and ahead of us is the deep gully of **Sharplow Dale**. The path deviates east to round the head of the dale, following the wall, before resuming its north-west course.

It's worth descending a short distance left where path crosses a ruined wall, to look over the edge of the crags, revealing views of **Rocky Bunster** ridge, **Lover's Leap** and **Jacob's Ladder** rocks left and the **Narrows** right, with **Ilam Rock** and the foot of **Hall Dale** to the right.

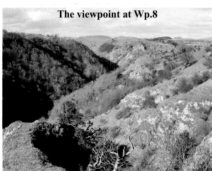

The viewpoint at Wp.8

Before returning to the path we traverse northwards along the top of the crags, coming to a rocky tor with cliffs on three sides, accessed by a narrow grass ridge; a radical viewpoint, but not for vertigo sufferers (Wp.8 80M). Climbing back to the path, we continue north to a corner in the wall and follow the path down the zigzags into the side valley ahead.

A gate in a wall (Wp.9 90M) takes us onto the path on the opposite side, which crosses a ridge following the wall on our right. It descends on its far side, reaching a right angled bend in the wall (Wp.10 96M).

Alternative route 1
Continue on the path, descending through **Upper Taylors Wood** to **Dove Holes**, then follow the tourist path back, to return via **Stepping Stones** (see Walk 6): 5.6 miles/9 km, 3 hours.

We turn right and follow the wall (NE) on a pathless ascent, climbing steeply at first. Heading north along a ridge, we enjoy views across **Dovedale** and **Hall Dale** opposite, and where the wall turns east we do so too, keeping to the relatively flat ground between the wall and the imposing crags that fringe **Nabs Dale** on our left. Opposite are the hills of **The Nabs** and **Baley Hill**, which we'll ascend shortly. Our route alongside the wall curves round to follow a northerly line, following the rim of **Nabs Dale**, and we end up on a narrow ridge.

Alternative route 2
From Wp.11 take the footpath down **Nabs Dale** and follow the tourist path to return via **Stepping Stones**; 6.9 miles/11 km, 3½ hours.

Alternative route 3
Turn right after the stile and follow the footpath NE past **Hanson Grange Farm**. Where several paths meet, turn right on the footpath leading to **Spend Lane**, which leads to **The Dog and Partridge**; 5.6 miles/9 km, 3 hours.

Staying close to the wall, we follow it down to the footpath beside a gate in **Nabs Dale** (Wp.11 120M), with the large farm of **Hanson Grange** on the far side.

Ignoring the stile, we head west instead across open ground behind the 'Access Land' sign on the opposite side of **Nabs Dale**, and climb steeply to the summit of **The Nabs**; there are splendid views over the whole of the southern Peak District, particularly across **Alstonefield** and **Wetton**, and down the dale towards **Dove Holes** and **Hall Dale**. On the opposite side of the dale to the north-west is an amphitheatre-like feature, a small section of **Dovedale** as it was before the ice ages; a much shallower, gentler valley. The floodwaters of the ice ages cut the deep gorge through the bend in the river, leaving this section high and dry.

We follow the ridge (NW) along a series of knolls, and cross a fence at a stile (Wp.12 130M) to reach the top of **Baley Hill**, with more views in all directions. Following the ridge (NNW), we descend to cross a ladder stile into a large area of pasture (Wp.13 135M).

Milldale, from Hanson Toot

Although we are now leaving access land, the stile and a well-used path running north-west towards **Milldale** indicate that a permissive route exists (if in doubt, stay on the dale side of the fence and follow it across steeper ground). We follow a generally NNW course, pass a dewpond, and return to the daleside access land by an open gateway in the wall on the left. Keeping the wall on our right, we emerge above **Milldale** at **Hanson Toot** viewpoint (Wp.14 160M), with **Viators Bridge**, the cottages of **Milldale** and behind, **Hope Dale** below. For refreshments at **Polly's Cottage**, descend the zigzag path, pass the National Trust sign, cross **Viators Bridge** and head into **Milldale** (Wp.15 165M).

Alternative Returns from Wp.15
We have several options. We could return via the tourist path (Walk 8, return leg) along the foot of **Dovedale**, or use parts of Walks 8 and 10 to create other variants.

Our return takes us back via **Shining Tor** and **Tissington**. To follow this, we return up the zigzag path behind the National Trust sign to **Hanson Toot**, keeping to the main path beyond Wp.14 and then staying beside the wall on the left.

At the top of the rise we cross a stone stile and follow the path along the dale rim in a north-east direction which leads to the distinctive rock headland of

Shining Tor, overlooking **Lode Mill** (see photo over page) (Wp.16 187M). From here the path heads east south-east along the rim of a side valley with **The Pinch** lane running along it. We come to a junction of paths (Wp.17 195M); right is signposted 'Tissington' but involves walking for a way along the A515, of which more later. Instead we continue ahead, following the wall, then joining the lane we saw earlier.

Overlooking Lode Mill

We follow this lane on the same heading (ESE) until a T-junction. Great care is required here: the road in front is the busy and fast A515 **Buxton** to **Ashbourne** road. Do not cross here, but walk along the wide verge on the right for 100 m, keeping away from the road to reach another road junction with better views of the traffic each way (Wp.18 200M). Crossing carefully, we take the path opposite to pass under the old railway bridge, taking the stone stile and wooden steps immediately after on the right to reach the old **Buxton** to **Ashbourne** railway, now the **Tissington Trail** footpath/cycleway - the unusual black footpath signs along the trail are made from recycled plastic.

These old railway tracks are usually too flat, and too often hidden in cuttings for great walking, but this section passes through attractive countryside. We turn left and head along the trail (SE), curving left over an embankment and running east under a bridge and through a deep rock cutting, at the end of which a footpath crosses, leading up from the secretive **Bletch Brook** valley on our left and crossed only by footpaths offering many pleasant summer walks. We stay on our route, curving through another cutting and under another bridge, which we then need to cross; at a footpath sign we turn left and follow the rim of the cutting up to the end of the bridge (Wp.19 237M).

Alternative route 4
At Wp.18, turn right and follow **Spend Lane** to **The Dog and Partridge**; 8¾ miles/14 km, 4½ hours.

We turn left across the bridge towards **Crakelow Farm** and through its yard to cross a wooden stile on the far side, then follow a faint tractor track across the field to another stile at the crest of the ridge. Passing to the left of a pond, we go through two wicket gates and through a small plantation with memorial plaques by some of the trees, then follow the path downhill (notice the evidence of ancient ridge and furrow cultivation) towards **Tissington**.

Two more stiles and a narrow alleyway beside a tiny cottage bring us to a lane; we bear right and enter **Tissington** at a road junction (Wp.20 252M).

Tissington is famous for its Whitsun well-dressing tradition when the six village wells are decorated with biblically-inspired panels of flower petals and clay.

The ceremony's origins are obscure; probably a tribal pagan rite taken over by early Christians, then finally reinvented as a faux-rural ceremony by the Victorians. Though its authenticity may be in doubt, there's no doubting the villagers' creativity and the colourful pageant of the dressed wells. The geology giving rise to the wells is complex; groundwater in the limestone is forced to the surface by a combination of impermeable shales and upfaulted lava, providing the wholesome groundwater that sustained Peak District communities before the arrival of a piped water supply.

Hands Well, the first of them, is on our right as we meet another lane. As we approach the village centre, **Children's Well**, dressed by local primary school children, is on the right, followed by the large **Hall Well** by a Yew tree on the left opposite **Tissington Hall**, home of the FitzHerberts - a rather gloomy rectangular building that wouldn't be out of place in a Tom Sharpe novel!

Hands Well

Yew Tree Well

After passing the tea shop, we bear left at the triangular green, passing the pond on our right, and following the road east past **Town Well** on the left. Past a small wooded area, we turn left at a road junction and come to the small **Coffin Well** on the right, opposite a squeeze stile through which we pass (Wp.21 260M) before the butcher's shop and well-kept little cottages facing the back lane. We return to the triangular junction and continue west to **Yew Tree Well**, notable for the Yew tree (what else) growing out of the top.

Just past the well (Wp.22 270M) we take a footpath on the left across the fields which runs alongside a wall to reach the **Tissington Trail** by an old railway bridge. We rejoin the trail, bearing right and crossing the A515 on a new footbridge, then go through **Fenny Bentley** cutting, rich with rare flowers in spring. A short embankment at the end of the cutting takes the trail over **Wash Brook**, and we come to the old **Thorpe Station**, now a picnic area (Wp.23). Turning right along the old station road, we reach **Narlows Lane** in sight of **The Dog and Partridge**, the end of our walk, and refreshment (Wp.1 300M).

10 THE OTHER DOVEDALE :
Hartington, Wolfscote Dale & Alsonefield

Strictly speaking, **Dovedale** only begins at **Viators Bridge** in **Milldale**. The course of the **River Dove** as it flows from **Hartington** to **Milldale** carries many names; **Beresford Dale**, **Wolfscote Dale**, **Coldeaton Dale** - but most are happy to consider it as part of **Dovedale**. We cover the whole of the dale between **Hartington** and **Milldale** with this route, taking in **Alstonefield** and the nature reserve of **Biggin Dale** as well, and including the splendid National Trust owned viewpoint of **Wolfscote Hill**.

This long route - 11.9 miles/19km if done in one go - can just as easily be done as two separate walks each of around 6.25 miles/10km thanks to its figure of 8 configuration, starting in **Hartington** or **Alstonefield**; or 'bus out, walk back', using the 442 bus from **Hartington** to **Alsop** old station.

The busy village of **Hartington** serves both as a tourist honeypot and a centre for rural services, offering a range of facilities for visitor refreshments. Much of the Stilton cheese sold in Britain is made here, and a visit to the cheese shop on the village green is well worthwhile (preferably after the walk - after 6 hours in a rucksack the cheese would be doing the walking!). The rest of the shops in the village, catering for the coach party trade, are pretty cheesy too, but the imposing three-storey **Gregory's** grocery shop (1836) is worth a look. It benefitted from the prosperity brought to the village by lead mining, and once sold gunpowder for blasting from a barrel, along with the usual boiled sweets, bread and broccoli. This led to a tragedy in the late 1800s when youngsters making 'fizz-bangs' with the gunpowder, spilled a little too much - causing one fizz-bang to set off the whole barrel of gunpowder, blowing themselves up and taking the roof off the shop.

The top of **Wolfscote Hill** provides one of the best viewpoints in the region, though its owner, the National Trust, seems coy about its status; we're at the hilltop before we even see a National Trust sign. It was to have been defined as Right to Roam access land, but this was rescinded; however, the National Trust who own it, allow walkers to access the summit by the route described here..

Safety Advice: 1. Limestone rock is slippery when wet, particularly on well-used paths. 2. Take care ascending/descending the dale sides, and on **Peaseland Rocks**: steep slopes, sheer cliffs, risk of vertigo, not recommended in hill fog.

Alternative start/finish Milldale or **Alsop** old station (in both cases, ensure car secure and belongings hidden); **Alstonefield**.

Access by bus: Nº442 **Ashbourne-Buxton**: 2 hourly service, 7 days, to **Hartington**.

Short versions	Access by car: A515 (Ashbourne-Buxton) to Newhaven, then B5054 to Hartington. Park in the free spaces in the village square or in the car park opposite Rooke's Pottery. Note: avoid taking cars along the lane from Hartington to Wolfscote Grange as there are no passing bays, car parking or turning facilities.
Hartington - Wolfscote Hill - Wolfscote Dale - Biggin Dale - Hartington (2 walker, 6¼ miles/10 km, 3 hours) **Alstonefield - Peaseland Rocks - Iron Tors - Shining Tor - Milldale - Alstonefield** (3 walker, 6¼ miles/10 km, 3 hours)	

Starting by the bus stop in the village square (Wp.1) we follow the B5054 south-west past the **Charles Cotton Hotel** and **Rooke's Pottery.** The alleyway between the pottery and the public toilets is the inauspicious start to our path running down **Dovedale**; we pass through a gate and follow the well-marked path south, crossing a track and passing through several fields. As we descend towards woodland, Charles Cotton's fishing lodge (no public access) can be glimpsed amongst Scots Pines by the river. His friend Izaak Walton found inspiration here for The Compleat Angler; the **Dove** remains a prime trout fishery.

The former hunting lodge of **Beresford Tower** is visible on the bluff ahead as we enter the wood. The path shortly crosses a footbridge and we pass the distinctive rock pinnacle overlooking **Pike Pool**, to walk alongside the river in the attractive wooded gorge of **Beresford Dale**.

We cross the **Beresford Dale Footbridge** by several large beech trees (Wp.2 22M) and follow the old trackway around the meadow's edge, then ascend through rocky ground to a gateway. Two tracks cross here (Wp.3 25M); we continue straight ahead uphill with a small wood on our right, passing a gateway with an old metal gate with views into the dale, then a track leading to a house on our right.

Beresford Dale Footbridge

Curving left, we reach a junction with a lane (Wp.4 36M) where we go right, uphill (SE) past a farm, the hillside on our left, to reach a shelter belt of trees and the wide gate entrance to National Trust land on **Wolfscote Hill** on our left (Wp.5 50M). Through the gate, we follow the gravel track, parallel with the trees, then turn due north uphill. As the track peters out we continue on the same heading to a line of stones - not a wall, as it first seems, but a natural outcrop of more resistant limestone - which we follow to the trig point with National Trust sign, at the crest of the hill (Wp.6 60M). Our reward is a panorama in all directions across the southern Peak District.

Retracing our steps to the gate (Wp.5), we head down the lane and past the farm to turn left (Wp.4) onto the track from **Beresford Dale**. When we reach the metal gate with the view, we pass through it onto access land on the far side. Crossing the dip, we reach the tree-covered tor opposite with an airy viewpoint of the dale below. The dale side is access land, and we could follow the rim of the dale south-west, but would have to drop back to the riverside where we meet a wall to avoid a hazardous descent amongst crags by the

The airy viewpoint before Wp.7

mouth of **Biggin Dale**. Instead, we descend through the dip behind the tor, past **Frank i'th' Rocks Cave** on our right and to the riverside (Wp.7 90M). The path follows the river's east bank on a pleasant amble along the dale (SE), bringing the crags of **Drabber Tor** and **Peaseland Rocks** into view on the right after passing a side valley. Note in particular a solitary standing stone-like pinnacle on a headland; we pass that way later. Passing through a stile where the **Biggin Dale** path comes in from the left (Wp.8/22 112M: turn left for shorter option to return to **Hartington**), we continue along the riverside, noting **Iron Tors** cave on the hillside to our left, to **Gipsy Bank** footbridge where our return route comes in (Wp.9/21 120M).

We pass gentler sloping ground on the opposite side of the river, traditionally used by Gipsies as a summer camp, our path following the river's twists and turns through this attractive and partly wooded dale, and passing **Coldeaton** footbridge (Wp.10 130M) to emerge through a 'dual carriageway' squeeze stile into **Lode Mill**, rich with snowdrops in spring.

By **Lode Mill Bridge** (Wp.11 148M) we climb through a stile onto the road - with care - and pass through the wicket gate opposite, signed for 'Shining Tor' (alternatively, cross the bridge and take the roadside path along the valley to **Milldale**). The **Shining Tor** path runs parallel with the road (SE) to a National Trust sign from where it climbs a steep defile to a junction of paths (Wp.12 162M). Turning right, we follow the wall until it turns left, then head north for a few yards to reach **Shining Tor** (Wp.13 170M) with views over **Lode Mill** and up the valley towards **Gipsy Bank**. We continue alongside the wall, eventually crossing a stone stile and descending the well-worn path down **Hanson Toot**, across **Viators Bridge** and into **Milldale** (Wp.14 190M). Taking the lane past **Polly's Cottage** (pausing for refreshments?) we take a very narrow path on the left by the red telephone box climbing steeply through a wood, then across two fields, reaching flatter ground in view of **Alstonefield Church**. Our well-used path crosses meadowland to rejoin **Millway Lane**, to go past the church to the village green at **Alstonefield** with **The George Inn** opposite - an excellent opportunity for refreshment (Wp.15 210M).

We leave **Alstonefield** past the joinery shop in the old chapel, along **Lode Lane**. Ignoring the first track on the left, we pass the '30' sign and take the second track left past the Youth Hostel, signed 'Coldeaton Bridge' (Wp.16 219M). Our walled track goes through a dog-leg, then takes us to open access land at the dale's rim (Wp.17 235M). The path slopes steeply down, but we turn left to follow the wall along the dale's rim, climbing at first, and passing a gate on the left. Now it's necessary to move a little away from the wall and down the hill to gain a sheep path heading north to a group of three gates.

Taking the right hand one (or whichever isn't locked), we cross the dip to meet the footpath on the far side (Wp.18 246M) and follow the wall along the rim, arriving at a viewpoint on the ridge (Wp.19 252M). For vertigo sufferers, or if the wind is strong, this will suffice - but a few steps further on reveal a gate in a fence below, with the distinctive pinnacle glimpsed earlier on the far side. After a short, careful descent we pass through the gate onto the headland with the pinnacle; there are fine views of **Peaseland Rocks**, **Drabber Tor**, **Wolfscote Hill** and **Biggin Dale** (Wp.20 258M).

Retracing our steps to Wp.19, we descend south-east towards the dale, soon picking up the slippery stepped path to **Gipsy Bank** footbridge, descending with care to the bridge where we regain the riverside path (Wp.9/21 270M); for the short walk from **Alstonefield**, turn right here and follow the outward route to **Milldale**). To return to **Hartington**, we turn left through the stile (Wp.8/22 277M) and take the path right for **Biggin Dale**, stony and sometimes wet underfoot, but worthwhile as the dale is rich in birdlife and flowers, particularly in springtime. At a branch in the dale with a wood in front of us the path goes right, while we take a left at a junction of paths (Wp.23 310M), heading north-west through a gate and along the left hand branch of the dale to another junction of paths (Wp.24 315M), turning left again for the direct return to **Hartington**.

The direct route heading north-west is muddy for the first section, then becomes a surfaced lane to pass a group of barns, now dropping to a road junction in **Hartington**, the church visible ahead. Left and downhill takes us into the village, where a further left opposite **Gregory's** leads us into the square (Wp.1 360M). A range of tea shops and public houses offer refreshment in the village.

Hartington

11 DOVEDALE LINEAR WALK

There are several linear walks in Dovedale between **Thorpe** and **Hartington** that can be done as a 'Bus Out-Walk Back' route, based on sections of Walks 8, 9 and 10, taking advantage of the 442 **Ashbourne-Buxton** bus service. Though the distance between these two points is quite long, walks can be conveniently broken for refreshments at **The George** in **Alstonefield** or **Polly's Cottage** in **Milldale**, and there are pubs at either end (**The Dog and Partridge** at **Thorpe** and several pubs and a tea shop in **Hartington**) where shelter - and a pint or a cuppa - can be had whilst waiting for the bus.

One of several linear options is outlined here. Detailed walk descriptions and maps are as for Walks 8-10.

* bus out, walk back

Safety Advice: See individual walk descriptions

Access by bus: N°442 **Ashbourne-Buxton** service to **The Dog and Partridge** at **Thorpe**. Return on same service from **Hartington**.

Access by car (bus out, walk back): B5054 to **Hartington**. Park in the village square or the car park. Catch the N°442 bus out to **The Dog and Partridge** at **Thorpe** and walk back.

Alternative start/finish
Park at **Narlows Lane** car park, **Thorpe**. Take the N°442 bus out to **Hartington**, and walk back.

The Old Cheese Shop at Hartington

Start at **The Dog and Partridge** at **Thorpe**. Follow Walk 8 to **The George** at **Alstonefield** (Wp.18 180M). After rest and refreshment follow Walk 10 from Wp.15 to **Hartington**, choosing to finish the walk either via **Biggin Dale** or **Dovedale** between Wp.8/22 and **Hartington** (330M).

12 MINNINGLOW - 2000 Years of Industry

We walk through a hidden valley where man's contribution to the region's landscape over two millennia is particularly evident. Based mostly on the **Roystone Grange Archaeological Trail**, access land enables us to expand and amend this route to take in views across the dale as well as relics of the refractory brickmaking industry and the modern **Ballidon Quarry**.

The walk starts and ends on the **High Peak Trail**, originally the **Cromford and High Peak Railway** (1830), one of the earliest in the country, and actually the culmination of an earlier technology of horse drawn tramways connecting to the canal system. In fact, its engineer William Jessop originally hoped to build it as a canal, and the stations were called 'wharves'. Connecting the **Cromford Canal** with the **High Peak Canal**, it was the first engineered transport link across the Peak District, but was soon made technologically obsolete by newer locomotive-hauled railways. As it was horse drawn, the gradients had to be gentle, with cable haulage inclines (such as the one at **Middleton Top** near **Wirksworth**) provided at major level changes. For most of the route across the **White Peak**, it was built at the plateau level (325 m above sea level), but maintaining this level across lower ground at **Minninglow** required the construction of a drystone embankment, the largest unbonded masonry structure in Britain. The whole of the High Peak Trail is now a listed structure of historical interest.

Our route reveals traces of quarrying, lime burning and refractory brickmaking industries that followed the opening of the railway. Industrial scale lime manufacturing became a major part of the local economy two centuries ago with the coming of canals and their tramways and later, railways. Refractory brick making took advantage of unique local silica sand raw materials to supply heat resistant bricks for lining Sheffield's blast furnaces. Traces of earlier industry, from Roman times when lead was smelted, to the beginnings of agro-industry by the great pre-Reformation monasteries, are also found en route.

Safety Advice: Be alert for cyclists and off-road vehicles. If following the byway south-east of Wp.9, comply with quarry warning signs about blasting. Take care near the deep water at **Minninglow Silica Pit**.

Access by bus: Nº17 (**Chesterfield-Matlock-Warslow**, infrequent service, summer Sundays/bank holidays only) to **Pikehall**. Walk along the lane south of village, following instructions for car access.

Access by car: A5012 Via **Gellia Road** (**Newhaven** to **Cromford**) to **Pikehall**. At **Pikehall**, turn south along the lane, turning left immediately after old railway bridge. **Minninglow Wharf** car park (free) on left.

Access for cyclists: from **Wirksworth** or **Parsley Hay** via **High Peak Trail**.

Leaving the car park/picnic area (Wp.1) at its eastern end, we follow the **High Peak Trail** across a small lane and through a short cutting, on a left hand curve. The trail then crosses the low ground on the **Minninglow Embankment**, constructed entirely of dry stone masonry, including more recent repair work in keeping with the original historical listed structure. From the embankment, looking east, note how the route of the trail follows the contour of the hillside below the plantation on **Minninglow Hill**.

At the end of the embankment the trail bends right by an old limestone quarry, and heads south-east for around 1 km, passing through a rock cutting (note the ash trees growing out of joints in the rock), before reaching another old quarry (Wp.2 15M) where some of the features, including an old crane used to load stone into wagons, have been preserved. Beyond the quarry and another drystone embankment, is a former beehive limekiln on the left, in which lime was made by burning charcoal with limestone. A byway crosses the trail and just beyond, a grassy entrance on the right leads to well preserved remains of two refractory brick kilns (Wp.3 20M).

Retracing our steps to the byway crossing, we leave the **High Peak Trail** and turn (SE) onto the byway, **Gallowlow Lane**, through a stone stile beside a gate. Like many byways in this part of the Peak District, this is open to all traffic, so has sadly become a mudhole. Fortunately we turn right after 400 metres (Wp.4 30M) at a robust stone stile, and follow a footpath downhill (SW) past a dewpond and an old stone gatepost (with markings on it suggesting that it may be more ancient than its use as a gatepost implies) to a bridge under the trail (no direct link between the trail and the footpath here). Under the bridge we continue down the small valley to another robust stone stile in a wall to our left (Wp.5 40M).

View into the dale from Wp.6

Here we enter access land and head uphill (SSW), following the wall on our left. Where the wall levels, out we join a faint grass track, still parallel with the wall, with views over the dale and **Royston Grange Farm** to our right. When a rocky *tor* facing out over the valley comes into view, we head to it (Wp.6 50M).

In the foot of the dale we can see **Royston Grange Farm** and a more recent building, a bit chapel-like but in fact an old pump house. The rocks of the *tor* are yellower than normal limestone and are weathered into lumps and hollows, the result of the limestone being turned into dolomite by volcanic activity in the Carboniferous period.

To the south is a modern day successor to the quarries we saw earlier, the **Tarmac Ltd** quarry at **Ballidon** which forms a bowl to the south-west of the dale, with the screening and crushing plant at its south end. Quarrying and the National Park have an uneasy relationship and generate much controversy. Although intrusive in the landscape, large scale quarrying, along with farming, has provided a livelihood for Peak District communities long before the National Park was established - when we return, note how many stone-trucks are parked in **Pikehall**.

Though industrial quarries are not things of beauty, special landscape restoration techniques are used at **Ballidon**. On each face a final 'restoration blast' breaks up the artificial lines of the quarry face, and the top and bottom of the face are reshaped to mirror the rounded hill tops and scree foot slopes of the dales. Once quarries are worked out, the crushing plant taken away and the natural vegetation re-established, these artificial dales become havens for wildlife. Leaving the *tor*, we rejoin the grassy track and head south-east, parallel with the wall along the rim of the dale. Reaching a large dewpond after 400 metres (Wp.7), we join a track heading due west, running diagonally down the hill to a tarmac byway road at the bottom of the dale (Wp.8 60M). The rectangular rock cut in the far side of the dale was originally a blaster's shelter from a time when quarry blasting was an inexact science and rocks flew!

The chapel-like pumphouse Wp.9

Turning right (NW), we follow the byway road for 500 metres, passing through a gate by the chapel-like pump house (Wp.9), then through a gate into the field containing the pump house. This was used to pump compressed air through cast-iron pipes to rock drills in the quarries nearby.

To the north-west are the foundations of two much older buildings, a 12th century monastic grange, where lay monks farmed sheep for meat, fleece and sheepskin in early agro-industry.

Leaving the pump house, we continue up the byway through a gate and past the present day **Roystone Grange Farm**. Rough stonework at the foot of the farmhouse gable end shows that it is built on the foundations of a very much older building. Beyond the farmhouse a brick and render barn on the left has a signboard (Wp.10) describing Roman habitation in the valley. We can cross the stile by the waypoint and observe the marked out Roman farmstead, and wander at will on the hill (**Roystone Rocks**, access land) behind, returning to the same stile to get back to the byway. This continues for around a kilometre as it leaves the dale (ignore misleading 'private' signs on a cattle grid), reaching Wp.11 at 90M where the tarmac turns sharp left.

Here we turn right (ESE) along a track (**Minninglow Lane**), ignoring a farm track on the left and descending to a point with gates on both sides, the one on the left leading to a small parking area for anglers (Wp.12 100M) at **Minninglow** silica sand pit. Passing through the gate we take the indistinct path (E) up on to the bank, which shortly gives us a view of the deep water-filled pit. The silica sand came from sandstone rock that was laid down above the limestone around 180 million years ago, and was then completely eroded away, surviving only in collapsed caves and solution cavities in the limestone. The remains of the old brickworks lie amongst the Scots pines to the south, though there is no public access.

After returning to Wp.12 we continue east along **Minninglow Lane**, passing through a gate and turning north-east, following the fence around the silica sand pit. The track then turns 90 degrees right and (now **Gallowlow Lane**) heads south-east towards the **High Peak Trail**, the stone embankment we crossed earlier visible to the east below **Minninglow Hill** summit. This track brings us to the **High Peak Trail** (Wp.13 115M), the track crossing near the brick kilns of Wp.3. Here we turn left and retrace our steps to the **Minninglow Wharf** car park (Wp.1 135M).

the 'Stonehenge of the North', **Arbor Low** is amazingly understated. A
ll sign points the visitor up a concrete farm track to three parking spaces
an honesty box for the entrance fee (£1 per adult), then through a working
yard to reach the monument.

wever, once there the visitor will be grateful for this lack of development,
s situation on a high point on the windswept plateau is all the more
matic and atmospheric. Nobody really knows why it was built; the
orians muttered darkly about human sacrifices, but the modern theory is
it was a central meeting place for the local tribe to hold celebratory events.
ther words, it was a venue for booze-ups, a sort of Neolithic nightclub -
may be why the people who built it are called the Beaker Folk; they
yed a beer but hadn't got round to inventing the pint glass.

walk starts and finishes in the typical limestone village of **Monyash** and
ides a rare opportunity (footpaths being relatively few in number in this
) to experience the open spaces and big skies of the central plateau of the
ite Peak**, and also takes in the hidden **Cales Dale** and the upper part of the
hkill**. **Moynash** was formerly a centre for lead mining and Quakerism. It
offers refreshments in the form of **The Old Smithy Café** and **The Bull's
d Pub** (both facing the medieval market cross on the village green).

l on a warm spring or summer day, or for the more intrepid a bright snow
ered winter's morning, this route was researched (of course) on a wet
ober Sunday!

ty Advice: (1) Stone stiles and limestone rock underfoot are very slippery
et weather. (2) The section through upper **Cales Dale** (Wps.17 to 19) has
steep scramble sections with no well defined footpath and may be
grown with nettles and loose rocks underfoot. Less intrepid walkers
ld use the alternative route via **One Ash Grange Farm**. (3) Do not enter
s or mine workings in **Lathkill Dale**.

ess by bus: Nº177 **Bakewell-Monyash-
gg** (Mon-Sat); Nº181 (**Sheffield-
ewell-Hartington**) Sun/BH Mon (to
or Low Gate**)

ess by car: B5055 (**Bakewell**-A515) to
nyash**. Park in the small car park off the
dington Road** north of the village green
nobstructively on street.

Alternative start/finish
Lathkill Dale head (layby on B5055 by Wp.20); **Arbor Low** gate (Nº181 bus, ask to be let off at **Arbor Low**)
Admission charge to **Arbor Low** £1 per adult.

ting at the medieval market cross on the village green (Wp.1), we cross
35055 and head east for 100 metres, then turn right through a squeeze stile
the churchyard (Wp.2) to follow the path (S) along the edge of the

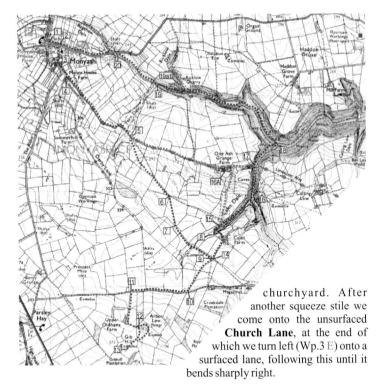

churchyard. After another squeeze stile we come onto the unsurfaced **Church Lane**, at the end of which we turn left (Wp.3 E) onto a surfaced lane, following this until it bends sharply right.

Here we continue east along a smaller lane and immediately after at a fork in the lanes we branch left, following the footpath sign for the **Limestone Way** (Wp.4 10M) along a sometimes muddy farm track.

Glimpses of the limestone gorge of **Lathkill Dale** are visible on the left as we continue (SE) along the path between stone walls. We pass over a stone stile by a gate and continue into a dip, now with open ground to our left and hummocky ground visible on the opposite side, then across another stone stile over the wall on the right and across the dip. Here we come to an old green footpath sign pointing ahead to 'Youlgreave' (Wp.5 25M). However, at this point we leave the **Limestone Way** footpath to take a less well-defined path on a more south south-east direction.

Navigation over the next few fields is difficult; the path is unclear, there are no waymarks, and the field boundaries vary from those shown on the OS Explorer map. We start by heading diagonally (SSE) across the field to the right of the electricity poles and look out for a stone stile on the horizon which we cross to continue on the same bearing across the fields and three more stiles until we get to a footpath sign (Wp.6).

Here we take the right fork, again heading diagonally (SSE) across the field, towards but a bit to the left of the strip of woodland at the southern end of the field, and when the corner of the field becomes visible, we make for it. This brings us (ignoring a field gate) to cross another stile (Wp.7 40M), then through a small hummocky field (old lead workings) to head due south-east towards a derelict stone stile to the right of two hawthorn trees. We then pass through a dip, following the remains of a stone wall to another stile (Wp.8) where the path continues alongside a stone wall (SE), until a farm track crosses the line of the wall (Wp.9).

Here we turn through 90 degrees to the right, not along the farm track but following a path (SW) along the bottom of a shallow valley under the power lines, through an old gateway and on to a stone stile (Wp.10). We turn right (W) to follow **Long Rake** road (take care as quarry traffic uses this road) for around 700 metres to a small brown sign on the left for 'Arbor Low' (Wp.11 60M) where we turn left and head due south along the concrete farm track, passing a small parking area to come to the 'honesty box' by **Upper Oldhams Farm** - see introduction. We continue through the farm buildings to a concrete stile, where the path to the monument turns to the south-east over a further concrete stile (Wp.12 75M) to **Arbor Low**.

The **Arbor Low** monument consists of a circular earthen bank, inside which is a ditch surrounding a level platform with a stone circle built on it: the stones are now lying flat but were probably originally standing. To appreciate the site in the context of its landscape, it's worth walking around the top of the earthen bank before crossing to the platform to look at the stones.

Leaving **Arbor Low** we head south-east to a concrete stile, crossing a shallow linear ditch, possibly a ceremonial way. Crossing the stile we head for the distinctive mound in the next field, **Gib Hill**, a circular flat-topped burial mound (Wp.13). The top of this mound is a fine viewpoint for the limestone plateau and on to the high ground around **Buxton**. The disturbed ground to the south is a silica sand pit that once supplied the **Friden** brickworks.

Cales Dale at 120 minutes

We retrace our steps back to Wp.9 to continue (NE) along the farm track, through an old gateway (Wp.14 105M) and on towards **Cales Farm**, then follow the track to the left of the farm as it curves through a small valley, leading to a wicket gate on the right into the Right to Roam land of **Cales Dale** (Wp.15 120M). Here we have a choice. Unless you're feeling intrepid, the best option is to stay on the track, heading almost due north, and follow the footpath (N) towards **One Ash Grange Farm** (Wp.16A), where we meet the **Limestone Way**. Here we can either turn left (W) for a quick return to **Monyash**, or right (E) to descend into **Cales Dale** and reach Wp.17.

However, the route through **Cales Dale** described below lets us experience some unmanaged Peak District countryside in almost complete solitude.

After passing through the wicket gate, we scramble carefully to the base of the valley and turn left. There is no formal footpath, but sheep paths lead us down the dale, which steadily becomes deeper between limestone crags.

We cross a fallen tree after 200 metres, and after a further 200 metres come to a tangle of fallen trees almost completely blocking the base of the dale. Rather than struggling through the fallen timber, we head right alongside a small wall.

The valley becomes considerably deeper at this point, as another valley joins it from the right, and we are above some low cliffs. We continue to the right and come to a point where a tree with two trunks grows in a gap in the cliffs below, used by sheep to ascend and descend. We descend, very slowly and carefully, and come to the point where the valleys meet and find a waymark post (Wp.16). Following sheep tracks down the dale, we then go through a gateway/stile to reach the **Limestone Way** (Wp.17 140M) which we ignore as we continue down the dale, now on a proper path, passing a powerful spring on our right.

Rounding a corner, we come face to face with the limestone cliffs of **Lathkill Dale**. We cross a wooden footbridge, and at the meeting of the paths turn left (NW) along the well-used path up the dale (Wp.18 145M). The path heads first north-wesr, then turns to east north-east as we pass the entrance to a blind dale to the right, below the prominent **Parson's Tor**. The unfortunate parson, the vicar of **Monyash** in 1776, returning on horseback from a heavy drinking session in **Bakewell**, rode too close to the cliff edge and was thrown from his horse to his demise.

The wooden footbridge

Lathkill Head Cave to our left, the source of the **River Lathkill**, should be admired from the outside, as evidenced by the fallen rocks in the cave mouth. We follow the path along the base of the dale, now dry, looking out for the rare Jacob's Ladder plant, and cross over a stone stile, until we come to a gate marking the end of the dale proper (Wp.19).

A short detour along a waymarked footpath to the right would bring us to a viewpoint overlooking the upper part of the dale (Refer to Walk 16 for the route description). Otherwise, we continue straight on along the base of the valley until the path reaches the B5055 (Wp.20 170M) by a toilet block where we cross carefully and walk (E) up its wide northern verge for around 600 metres to return to the market cross in **Monyash** (Wp.1 180M) and a choice of refreshments at the **Old Smithy** or the **Bull's Head**.

The gritstone plateau of **Stanton Moor** between **Matlock** and **Bakewell** is of little use for farming, so remains unenclosed, untamed and partly wooded, though it has been occupied by people since the Bronze Age. Relics include the **Nine Ladies** stone circle at the north end of the moor in a grassy glade surrounded by birch trees. This atmospheric, arguably supernatural place, has long been associated with the witches' art.

The gritstone that created the moor also gave a living to generations of quarrymen from surrounding villages such as **Birchover**; its fine stone was used in building the Houses of Parliament. The quarrying has nibbled away the edges of the moor, leaving rock faces and spoil heaps re-colonised by woodland and nature.

Modern day successors to this tradition present a dilemma, as proposals to reopen the **Endcliffe** and **Lees Cross** quarries on the east of the moor have raised determined opposition. The old quarries have been occupied by Eco-Warriors, and their ingenious structures and home made dwellings are an unusual feature of this walk. This walk shows both sides of the coin: modern quarrying would scar this landscape (though nature will ultimately repair the damage) but without work the quarrymen's descendants of villages like **Birchover** will drift away, and another Peak District village will be left to weekend cottagers and the Hanging-Basketocracy.

We begin in **Rowsley**, where the B6012 **Chatsworth** road leaves the A6. It has two pubs, a shopping centre and the imposing **Caudwell's Mill**, which produces organic stoneground flour and houses a craft centre. The route starts with a gently sloping climb along side of the **Derwent valley** to the Eco-Warrior camp at **Endcliffe**, before reaching the moor and the **Nine Ladies** stone circle. It takes us via the moor's eastern rim to **Birchover** and refreshments, then back to the moor and the stone circle before returning to **Rowsley**.

Safety Advice: Care needed near crags or quarry edges.

Access by bus: NºR61 or TransPeak (**Bakewell-Matlock**, frequent) to **Rowsley**; or Nº172 **Bakewell-Matlock** (Mon-Sat inc B/H Mon, 2 hourly) to **Birchover**.

Short Version
The section between **Birchover** and the stone circle can be done as a 5 km/1.5 hour route starting near **Birchover**. Follow the walk described from **Birchover** (Wp.16) to the stone circle (Wp.8) then from Wp.8 to **Birchover**.

Access by car: A6 to **Rowsley**: turn south onto the lane in the village signposted 'Caudwell's Mill'. Park in the car park by mill, or in the shopping outlet car park and walk to **Caudwell's Mill**. N.B. There may be restrictions and limited opening hours in either car park.

Alternative start/finish: Near **Birchover**, park in the layby near Wp.17. Little parking available in **Birchover** itself.

Leaving the car park at **Caudwell's Mill**, we turn south and cross the **River Wye** on a stone bridge. The lane bends sharply to the right but our path follows a farm road straight ahead along the floor of the **Derwent Valley**. The road starts climbing the side of the valley through a wood. Soon after a sharp left hand bend (Wp.2 20M) we follow a waymarked path through a kissing gate beside a rhododendron hedge, and through a field gate. We fork right and pass **Stanton Woodhouse Farm** on our right, then go through a metal gate (Wp.3 25M) and onto a grassy track that takes us round a hill.

Passing through a gateway with the **Earl Grey Tower** ahead on the horizon, the path forks left from the track and heads (SSW) onto a low ridge.

Through a small wooden gate, we come to a number of home-made tented and wooden habitations, some high in the trees: this is the Eco-Warriors camp (Wp.4). They tolerate walkers and we pass without hindrance. Looking over the old **Endcliffe Quarry** to our left, we can see the network of wires and towers they have constructed across the quarry, designed to make it impossible to evict them.

Eco-Warrior dwelling

Past the encampment, we reach a lane (Wp.5 40M) and turn right (NNW), forking left at a road junction (Wp.6) signposted 'Stanton in Peak'. This lane climbs around a shoulder of the hill and we take a waymarked footpath (Wp.7) on the left, climbing to enter a wood where we keep right, following the path along the fence until we cross it by a stile with a 'Marooned Hiker' sign (Wp.8 55M). Following the path on the other side (WSW), we cross a larger path and arrive in a glade surrounded by birch woods, the atmospheric setting for the **Nine Ladies** stone circle (Wp.9 60M). You may see covens of witches, but more likely, lots of other walkers.

When we leave the stone circle we head (ESE) directly towards the **Earl Grey Tower**, a somewhat ugly folly put up to commemorate Earl Grey and his great Reform Act of 1832. After crossing a stile (Wp.10) and passing the tower, stone steps take us down to a path by a National Trust sign where we turn right (SE) alongside a fence. After a few minutes the fence and the main path bend sharp right, but a few paces straight ahead brings us to the **Cat Stone** (Wp.11 70M), a good place for a break.

The path follows the fence for around 1 km, detouring to the moor edge (steep drops) for panoramic views over the **Derwent Valley** towards the county town of **Matlock**. As we round another promontory, a large lead smelting factory surrounded by poplars becomes visible. This was the **Millclose Lead Mine**, once the Peak District's largest, and workings ran right beneath **Stanton Moor**. Though the mine closed in 1942, its smelter survives by recycling car batteries from all over Europe.

Opposite the large **Gorse Stone** rock, and a viewpoint on the left, we cross a stile on the right by a National Trust sign (Wp.12 80M). We take the lower of the two paths leading from it, traversing the hillside in a south-west direction, then dropping down to a stile onto a lane (Wp.13).

We turn right and shortly left again onto a waymarked footpath to follow a field boundary on our left towards a farm. We continue past the farm, passing to the left of all farm buildings except one, and through one squeeze stile by a gate, followed immediately by another on the right (Wp.14 100M). The path now leads (W) along a track with a wooden rail fence on the left, to a lane (Wp.15) opposite an ugly quarry building where we turn west along the lane into **Birchover**.

Birchover is a compact village of small quarrymen's cottages huddled beneath a rocky ridge of gritstone. We pass a Wesleyan chapel, the village Pinfold (a pound for stray animals) and a Primitive Methodist chapel by a village well. Here as in South Wales, Primitive Methodism, mining and quarrying seem to go together. This village has not lost contact with its history and provides facilities for visitors without selling its soul to them. Near the end of the village street we come upon the two village pubs, **The Red Lion**, an honest pub that welcomes walkers, and further on, the slightly more upmarket **Druid Inn** at the foot of **Rowtor Rocks**, reportedly a sacred site for Druids.

As we reach **The Druid Inn**, we come upon a commemorative Millennium Stone. Before the stone, we take a waymarked footpath on the right (Wp.16 115 M), heading (NW) along the rocky ridge to the north of **Birchover**. The path rises through beech and oak woodland growing on waste rock tipped from old quarries. We emerge into a large (private) parking area, pausing to note two cleverly carved stones on either side of the path. Turning left on the lane (Wp.17) opposite a working quarry, we head NNE.

After around 300 metres a path by some boulders leads us into the woods on the right, heading NE then N, then meeting another path by a gate, which we go through and walk uphill to the distinctive **Cork Stone** at a junction of paths, its carved footholds and metal rungs allowing those more foolhardy than this author to climb it (Wp.19 130M). From Wp.19, we take the left-hand of two paths running NNE across the moor, passing west of the trig point, along the edge of a series of old quarries, with views to the west, then into a wooded area. At a junction of paths in a small clearing (Wp.20) we take the larger path to the right (ENE), ignoring the small path ahead, and fork right again where the path enters a shallow dip, bringing us back to the **Nine Ladies** stone circle (Wp.9) past the **Piper Stone**.

The Cork Stone

The route just before Wp.21

Leaving the stone circle on its north-eastern side, we turn left and follow the large path (NW) through three stiles/gates, to **Lees Road**, (Wp.21 170M). Turning left along the lane for around 100 metres and ignoring a quarry entrance on the right, we take a path on the right, just after the road enters **Sheepwalk Wood**.

The trick is to take whichever path takes us nearest to due north and downhill to the bottom of the wood. At the bottom of the wood we follow a path (NE) which descends steeply to a lane near some cottages. Turning right, we continue to a stone viewpoint on the left hand side of the lane (Wp.22 180M), giving a broad view of **Wyedale** and lower **Lathkill**, **Haddon Hall** and **Bakewell**.

Just after the viewpoint a waymarked footpath leads (N) across fields to the left, to another lane which we follow downhill to the hamlet of **Congreave**. The lane zigzags down the hill, and on the third hairpin bend (Wp.23) a footpath on the right takes us through a squeeze stile by a gate, and then contours around the hillside before dropping down to a stream. We pass through a wicket gate, cross the stream, then immediately go through another wicket gate on the right and through a corner of a small wood. The path angles diagonally across a field towards a line of trees, then follows them down to the side of the **River Wye**. The path then follows the river for a short distance until a lane comes in from the right (Wp.24).

We follow this lane along the side of the river past a playground (right), then cross the river on the stone bridge by the car park entrance (210M) where we started the walk. Before leaving a visit to **Caudwell's Mill** itself is worthwhile, particularly for home bakers who will appreciate the mill's stoneground flour.

15A & 15B LIMESTONE AND GRITSTONE from ELTON

These routes can be done either as two separate walks or one longer walk. Our base, the attractive village of **Elton**, is a former lead mining village that retains a particularly strong sense of community, despite the demise of lead mining. Its school, church, post office and village hall remain and, perhaps of more relevance to the visitor, **The Duke of York** pub and a café, but no public toilet (if there was, it would have to be called the Elton John).

Elton is a village of both limestone and gritstone, located as it is close to the geological boundary between the two rock types. Carboniferous limestone is found under the village itself and to the south and west, whilst to the north and north-east is the millstone grit formation, its hard, outcropping sandstone beds interspersed with softer, more easily weathered shale. This difference in rock type is reflected in the landscape, in landforms (rounded limestone hills with steep dales, compared with gentle valleys and steep gritstone *tors*), in field boundaries (stone walls compared with hedges), and plants (grasslands and hawthorn scrub, compared with rushes, bracken and oak woods). These clues indicate where the rock types change as we progress.

The walk is described as two separate walks, but the GPS waypoints and timings are provided as a single long route, as the 'linking' sections are lengths of lane where it is difficult to go wrong.

Combined walk

3 | 4¼ H | 8¾ miles/14km | 320m / 320m | 2

Access by bus: Nº172 **Matlock-Elton-Bakewell** (Mon-Sat inc BH Mon); No Sunday service.
Access by car: B5056 **Ashbourne-Bakewell** or B5057 to the cross-roads west of **Winster**, then the unclassified road west to **Elton**. Park unobstructively on street in the east end of the village where the road is wider.

Alternative start/finish: Layby on B5056 by Wp.22.

15A: LIMESTONE

This walk crosses a typical limestone landscape of dale and plateau, and though the gradients are gentle it is not without its challenges. Never was the expression 'dry valley' so misused as in the case of **Gratton Dale**. This is squelching, boots-and-gaiters, mudlarking at its best, and not for those that like to walk in sandals or trainers! However 'Mucky Dale' is a haven for birdlife, and after surmounting it some pleasant walking is to be had. There are a couple of surprises, too, in the shape of two sculptures, part of a Millennium project by Middleton and Smerrill Parish Council to mark the parish boundary with inscribed stones or sculptures (see www.sitesofmeaning.co.uk).

Safety Advice: Slippery conditions in **Gratton Dale**.

We start (Wp.1) at the junction of **Moor Lane** and **Main Street** (named with tongue in cheek - it's the only street in **Elton**), with **The Duke of York** to our left and the church to the right. Heading east, we pass **Westgate Cottage**, bearing a blue plaque for Alfred Gregory, the photographer on the 1953 Everest expedition. At the end of a village we come to a junction of lanes (Wp.2 5M).

Dale End Farm

Ignoring the track leading ahead into the farm, and the old finger post pointing west (the footpath shown on the OS map heading for **Gratton Dale** is lost amongst mud and heaps of waste tipped in the farmyard) leaves a choice of lanes; sharp right is **Cliff Lane**, while we head north-west on the pleasant, quiet **Gratton Lane** into a broad valley, past **Dale End Farm** until we see a red phone box on the left (Wp.3 20M).

Both signs on the left point us to the **Gratton Dale** path. After 200 metres we pass through a gate at the mouth of the dale by a well-preserved beehive lime kiln on the right, where the mudlarking begins, continuing unremittingly for the next mile or so. Some respite can be gained by following cattle tracks along the western slope of the dale, but this trades mud for hawthorn spikes, and we have to descend back into the mud to pass through two gates. After the second gate the path switches to the left of a tumbledown wall; by now the worst of the mud is over. We should not let the mud of 'Mucky Dale' distract us from what is after all a nature reserve. During the research we heard owls, and a sparrowhawk was hovering over the dale in search of prey.

We continue (SSW) to a gate in a wall (Wp.4 60M) where the dale splits into two branches; we turn right and go through another gate, heading along **Long Dale** (WNW). There is relatively dry and pleasant walking on springy grass along the foot of the dale, but we can follow an alternative green track up the right hand side of the dale before returning to the foot of the dale. Following the dale, we pass through a gate (Wp.5 70M), pausing at the small walled enclosure on our left which houses a sculpture comprising three standing stones with a sun, three birds and the words 'We meet to create memories and depart to cherish them' carved in the stone. They must go to more worthwhile meetings than I do - but as the text was apparently taken from a menu in a cafe at the base of Everest, perhaps that's not surprising.

The path then follows the wall on its opposite side before climbing out of the dale on a north-west bearing, looking back to admire the dale's attractive shape, and the distinctive hummocks on the opposite side that indicate former lead mining. We pass through a field gate in the wall facing us (Wp.6 80M), with **Youlgrave** visible in the distance, and a distinctive group of trees on the hilltop to the right, then head parallel with a wall on our right (NNE) and through a gate, following a shallow valley through several gates to a slightly overgrown path between two walls which takes us, on a bend, to **Weaddow Lane** (Wp.7 110M).

Turning right we follow it (E) along an avenue of ash and sycamore. Past **Smerrill Grange Farm**, the road bends right and left to cross a small side valley; the hummocks in the field to the left mark the site of the abandoned medieval village of **Smerrill**. Beyond in the foot of the valley, a line of limestone cliffs marks the route of a gorge, (no public access) where the stream has eroded a shallow-sided valley right through the shales in the Millstone Grit formation and then cut a steep gorge into the harder limestone below. Above, on the far side of the valley, is the gritstone rock outcropping.

On the right of the lane at the second bend (Wp.8), we come across an unexpected sight: the second sculpture, a cubic block of sandstone carved into two new-age style faces and four flowers, the eyes in the faces and the flowers formed from small glazed ceramic tiles. A verse is carved into the rock: 'To see the world in a grain of sand, in the palm of your hand and, eternity in an hour, and heaven in a wild flower'. Right on! The lane soon descends into the valley to a road junction by a B&B called the **Gratton Cheese Factory** (Wp.9 140M).

To complete this walk and return to Elton, turn right, and in around 300 metres pass the red telephone box at Wp.3, retracing our steps to the start (Wp.1 165M).

Alternatively, to continue on the Gritstone part of the walk, turn left and follow the directions given below from Wp.9.

15B GRITSTONE

This walk provides a gentle introduction to gritstone country and the opportunity to visit the distinctive gritstone *tor* at **Robin Hood's Stride**. Although mostly easy going, exploring the rocky hill before reaching the *tor* can involve some difficult going through shoulder high bracken.

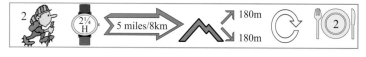

Safety Advice: 1. Take care if you're tempted to scramble on **Robin Hood's Stride**. 2. Avoid the route through bracken in July and August as the spores may be harmful.

We follow Walk 29A to Wp.2, where we have a choice. If we turn sharp right on **Cliff Lane** we'll reach Wp.13 in 10 minutes and shorten the walk by 40 minutes. For the full walk we take **Gratton Lane**, following Walk 29A as far as Wp.3 but instead of turning left at the red phone box, we continue along the lane to the road junction by the **Gratton Cheese Factory** house (Wp.9 20 M/140 M for combined walk).

We take the lane to the right which climbs the opposite side of the valley;

notice the change in vegetation, rushes in the fields indicating poorly drained soils on the shales of the Millstone Grit formation. We stay on the lane until a hairpin bend to the left (Wp.10 30M/150M) where we continue straight ahead (E) on a stone track, passing a painted sign for 'Rock Farm', and a piece of round gritstone with 'Spout House' carved in it. About 150 metres past a house, the track splits into two; we take the less used, left hand fork (Wp.11).

We pass through a series of gates, all tied with baler twine and continue across the next field, through a gateway and where the track bends off to the left (Wp.12) we continue on a path (E), over a stile in a modern fence, passing between two young oak trees and (ESE) through four small fields with tumbledown walls, with views along **Gratton Dale** and across to **Smerrill Grange** on the opposite side of the valley. We eventually find ourselves heading south, following a derelict stone wall to the corner of a field by a number of large rocks, showing diagonal 'current bedding'. We cross the stile and pass a large spoil heap on the left (an old quarry now owned by a motorbike scrambling club) and follow the path (SE), emerging on **Cliff Lane** at Wp.13 (50M/170M), by a seat next to a series of stone troughs. We turn left and uphill for around 700 metres until we come to a bracken-covered hill on the right and a public footpath sign by a telegraph pole (Wp.14).

Now the route involves some arduous pathless walking through neck-high bracken though this can be avoided either by turning right, following the track, then turning left on an overgrown track around to **Robin Hood's Stride** at Wp.16, or by continuing on the lane until it's crossed by the **Limestone Way** footpath, then turning right onto the well-marked footpath to Wp.18.

If not tempted by the alternatives, leave the lane and head east north-east (on access land) into the bracken and follow sheep tracks to the top of the prominent rock scarp, which we follow without too much difficulty to two small pools in the rock on the edge of the scarp (Wp.15). These may

Excellent views from Wp.15

be swirl holes formed in a river bed, illustrating how much erosion has taken place since these rocks were uplifted from the bed of the sea. There are good views across to **Elton** and to **Robin Hood's Stride**.

From Wp.15 the way lies across a sea of tall bracken. We head due east towards the end of the ridge and then turn north-east, heading downhill towards an area of oak woodland to the right of the **Stride**, making what use we can of sheep tracks through the bracken, and keeping away from the quarry to the north-west. The going is slightly easier once in the oak trees, and in due course we come to a track running alongside a stone wall which leads us to a gate (Wp.16 75M/195M), right under the **Robin Hood's Stride**. Through the gate, we turn left, following the wall (WNW) until we pass through a gateway, when we turn north-east and reach the top of the ridge, below the **Stride**, at Wp.17. The two high pillars, distinctively eroded, give the rocks their name, as Robin Hood is reputed to have stepped between them. Take great care if you choose to climb on the rocks.

We head north-east and cross a stile (Wp.18) in the corner of the field by a number of gates, entering the field opposite by a gate and crossing it (ENE) to a stile over a fence, which takes us to **Cratcliffe Tor**, an area of bracken and large rocks (Wp.19). We are heading for the aptly named **Hermit's Cave**, inhabited in the 18th Century by a hermit sponsored by the local lord of the manor. We head to the right, picking our way along the foot of the rock face amongst several large rocks until we reach two large yew trees (Wp.20 90M/210M) behind which is a stone wall and a steel gate.

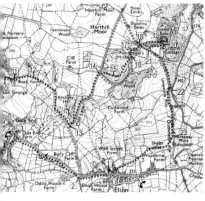

The rock faces are frequented by the rock climbing fraternity, with free climbing (they do it without ropes, not because they're tight or broke) particularly popular. We return to the fence, another stile taking us into a wooded sloping area. A small path takes us diagonally down the slope and through the wood until we emerge through another stile by a black painted seat with the words 'Hilary's Seat' forming its backrest (Wp.21).

We continue down the clearly visible **Limestone Way** footpath, following it to the base of the valley and through a gate at Wp.22 onto **Dudwood Lane** that runs up the opposite side of the valley, part of the prehistoric **Portway**, a trackway that ran from south to north across the Peak District. We climb about halfway up the hill on this lane until we turn right at a footpath sign (Wp.23 115M/235M).

This footpath heads slightly to the right of the large trees on the top of the hill, and a particularly muddy section follows a hedge for a while, though by staying to the south of this we can avoid the worst of it. We follow the electricity wires into the village, passing through a squeeze stile and into a dip, heading all the time west south-west towards the church. As we approach the church we pass some modern houses to our right and go through a small junkyard of abandoned cars before entering the churchyard. Following the path around the edge of the churchyard rings us back at the start of our walk (Wp.1 135M/255M). Having been marched up to the top of the hill and marched back down again, you may consider the pub opposite, **The Duke of York**, rather well named!

Lathkill Dale and **Bradford Dale** meet at **Alport**, south of **Bakewell** near **Youlgrave**. With their pure, clear spring-fed streams, they are havens for wildlife. The walk along **Lathkill Dale** is well known and described in many guides, but all too often the return leg seems to have been an afterthought, so that the second half of the walk becomes just a trudge back to the car: and whilst the lower part of **Bradford Dale** is popular as a Sunday afternoon stroll, many people turn back before reaching the more interesting upper part of the dale.

This walk takes in both dales on a figure of 8 route, first traversing the length of **Lathkill Dale** from **Alport** to **Monyash** and returning via the northern rim of the dale, before dropping back into the dale and crossing the outward route. From this point, the walk follows the **Limestone Way** over **Calling Low** and then a lane leading to **Middleton-by-Youlgrave**, dropping down to the top end of **Bradford Dale** before traversing its length to return to **Alport**. It's a classic if long Peak District route when done in one go; 21 km if refreshments are taken in **Monyash**. However, it's quite gentle in terms of gradients, with only one steep uphill section, and there are a number of shorter variants.

Opportunities for refreshment are limited on the walk itself, though **Over Haddon** and **Monyash**, each a short distance off the walk, have pub and café facilities: there is nothing in either **Middleton** or **Alport**. **Youlgrave** (the correct spelling) is too congested, and you'll grieve if you try to park there.

*21 km if **Monyash** included   **most off route

Safety Advice: Stone stiles and limestone rock underfoot are very slippery in wet weather. Do not enter caves or mineworkings in **Lathkill Dale**.

Access by bus: Nº171 **Bakewell-Youlgreave** (Mon-Sat) or Nº181 **Sheffield-Bakewell-Hartington** (Sun/BH Mon), to **Alport**, or Nº177 **Bakewell-Monyash-Flagg** (Mon-Sat) to **Monyash**.

Shorter Options
The top and bottom loops of the figure of 8 could be done as two separate walks starting at **Monyash** and **Alport** respectively. **Lathkill Dale** could be done as a linear walk (though not on Sundays) by starting in **Bakewell**, taking a bus to **Alport**, walking to **Monyash** and getting a bus back to **Bakewell**. Sections of either dale could be done as 'there and back' walks.

Alternative start/finish Lathkill Dale head (layby on B5055 by public toilets, walk down dale to Wp.11); **Moor Lane** top (Wp.21).

Access by car: A6 to **Youlgrave** turn near **Haddon Hall**, then follow the B5056 and then the unclassified road towards **Youlgrave**. Park in one of the two small car parks at **Alport** (at the bottom of the hill up to **Youlgrave**) or unobtrusively on the roadside.

.We start opposite the red phone box in **Alport** (Wp.1), through a squeeze stile by a gate, waymarked to 'Conksbury'. The path heads (NW) through a small paddock and another gateway, then alongside a plantation on the right, We follow the path along the base of the wide valley through eight squeeze stiles or gateways, and past **Raper Lodge** on our left. Through a wicket gate, we cross a track (Wp.2 10M) and carry straight on (NNW) through a gate to arrive at a lane (Wp.3). Noting the hummocky appearance of the field opposite where the abandoned village of **Conksbury** once stood, we turn right and follow the lane down to and across the medieval **Conksbury Bridge**.

Shortly afterwards (Wp.4 15M) we take the path up the dale on the left, heading north-west. After a while the path leaves the river side, ascending the side of the dale and providing good views of the river and the cliffs opposite. The path, now heading west, drops back to the dale floor and arrives at a ford where birdlife, including the rare dipper, may be seen (Wp.5 30M).

The lane on the right zigzags steeply up to **Over Haddon**, where refreshments can be taken (0.7 km off route). To follow our path, we start along this lane but almost immediately turn left along a concession track through a gate, a sign informing us that we are entering the nature reserve. After around 10 minutes the path runs alongside a small channel, which emerges from an opening beneath the path - a *sough*, or drainage tunnel, for the **Mandale Lead Mine**. Opposite, a path leads right through the trees to the ruined **Mandale Lead Mine** engine house (Wp.6 40M), where the old mine shafts and surface workings are hidden amongst the trees, a notice board describing the history of the mine workings. Returning to the path by the river we continue upstream, passing a new wooden bridge (Wp.7) leading to the ruined **Bateman's House**, conserved by English Nature.

... we pass a small waterfall ...

We continue up the dale through **Palmerston Wood** and across a small meadow at the foot of a side dale (Wp.8 70M). (The small side dale to our north makes an attractive detour). The character of the dale changes again, with fewer trees, the path narrowing as it crosses the foot of scree slopes from the limestone crags above. We pass a small waterfall, where the river flows across a layer of tufa precipitated from springs in the valley floor. Five hundred metres further on, the dale bends to the north-west and **Cales Dale** comes in from the south-west by a footbridge (Wp.9/18 90M).

This is the point where the two loops of the figure of 8 meet. If only doing the lower loop, turn left here across the bridge. Otherwise, continue straight ahead up the dale.

Along this section the river is fed by many springs, though in summer or autumn may be dry altogether. The dale is now almost completely clear of trees and for the next kilometre we have an open walk along the base of the dale between limestone cliffs. The path shortly bends to the west, a blind dale running to the north, and passes between **Lathkill Head Cave** on the south and **Parson's Tor** (see Walk 13) on the north, the dale becoming narrower and

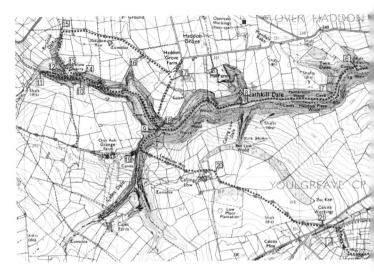

rockier. Passing a fenced off area where the rare Jacob's Ladder plant is protected, we go through a squeeze stile and into a more densely wooded area (Wp.10). A set of narrow stone steps on the right, steep and poorly maintained, lead to the viewpoint at Wp.14, if you feel like chancing a short cut. We, however, continue along the main path up the dale for around 300 metres when we pass through a gate and out of the dale into a broad, shallow valley (Wp.11 120M). A low wooden post with green waymarkers indicates that several footpaths meet here.

For refreshments in Monyash (an extra 1km each way), continue straight on at this point to meet the B5055, then turn left into the village (see Walk 13).

If not going to Monyash we turn sharp (almost 180 degrees) right (E) to follow the concessionary footpath leading above the rim of the dale.

Lathkill Dale, from Wp.14

A series of similar wooden posts point the way to the first viewpoint (Wp.12), then into a side dale (Wp.13) where we turn right through a gate to follow the waymarked route through the disused quarry to the second viewpoint (Wp.14 130M), a good picnic spot with views over the whole of the upper part of **Lathkill Dale**. This quarry was worked for the ornamental 'Figured Marble' Crinoidal limestone used in fireplaces in **Chatsworth House**.

Retracing our steps to Wp.13, we then head north along **Ricklow Dale**, crossing a robust stone stile then following a wall on our left. After around 500 metres we come to a stone stile on the left with a footpath signpost (Wp.15 135M) and turn right (E) on a grassy path up a short rise. After crossing two stone stiles the path turns east south-east. Crossing another four stone stiles,

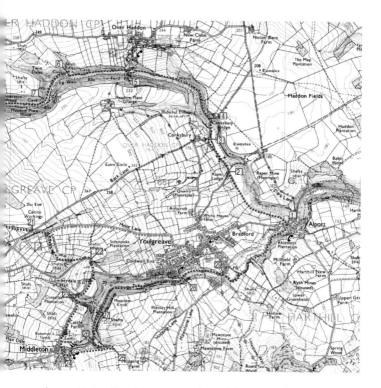

we descend into a dip with an extremely muddy gateway in front of us. To the right of the gateway, however, is yet another stone stile which we cross and head for the barn on the opposite side of the dip (SW), soon noticing another stone stile (Wp.16) where at the choice of paths we go right, still heading SW, roughly parallel with a line of electricity poles towards a line of trees. At the corner of two walls and another stone stile we cross a horse paddock on the same heading to reach a junction (Wp.17) where we turn right and head south south-west, crossing two stiles, and descending gradually to a gate with a signboard at the rim of the dale.

After taking in the views, we descend the steep zigzag path to the foot of the dale (Wp.9/18 175M). We cross the wooden bridge and follow the path along **Cales Dale**, shortly passing a strongly flowing spring on the left, then reaching the **Limestone Way** footpath crossing the dale (Wp.19). We turn left through a wooden stile, and are confronted with the 'Endless Staircase', the only steep climb on this walk. There's nothing for it but to make the ascent, arriving at a kissing gate at the top and pausing for the views across the dale.

The path rises (ESE) to the wooded top of **Calling Low**, passing to the north of the farm buildings, through six more kissing gates (watch out for sore lips!)(Wp.20 200M). Here the path bends to the right for a short while then returns to east south-east. After passing through the corner of **Low Moor Wood**, our well-used path crosses several fields before meeting a lane close to a layby (Wp.21 225M). Diagonally opposite we take **Moor Lane**, past the Peak District car park on the right, and turn right on a waymarked footpath heading past a picnic area (SSE) with sweeping views to the east, then cross a stile and, descending, turn east at the far side of the field.

The path meets a road at a sharp bend; we turn left, following the road round the bend, then take a footpath on the right (Wp.22) to head south through attractive parkland down the hill to a lane, where we turn right.

To shorten the walk from Wp.22, take **Moor Lane** into **Youlgreave**, then **Mawstone Lane** SE from the church to Wp.29.

The lane heads past **Lomberdale Hall** on our right, then round a sharp bend (the squeeze stile left just after the bend is a short cut to Wp.27). The seat built into the drystone wall just past this stile bears the text, "In quietness and in confidence shall be your strength", one of the parish marker stones for **Middleton** and **Smerrill** (see Walk 15A). Continuing on the lane, we pass a dairy farm and reach the attractive (though without facilities for walkers) little stone village of **Middleton** (Wp.24 255M).

Its main distinguishing feature is that it is (somewhat reluctantly) home to the biggest collection of Trabant cars outside East Germany. After the Berlin Wall fell (1989), they could be picked up for a song. It must have seemed like a good idea, but now these relics of Communist engineering rust in a farmyard to the left of the village square, some visible from **Trabant Corner** (Wp.24) as we turn down a track and head east.

We pass farm buildings on our right and immediately after, take a footpath across a stile to the right of the track (the track leads directly to Wp.26) following it downhill across fields, a plantation of Scots pines on our left, until we get to the foot of the valley where we cross a stone slab bridge across the stream (Wp.25). Carved into one slab is a verse by Alexander Pope: 'Consult the genius of the place in all; That tells the Waters or to rise or fall'; another parish boundary marker.

Turning left, we take a path above a line of low cliffs, then descend a set of steel steps to the valley floor, and cross a bridge. Passing a spring, we follow the path to turn right on a track by a complex network of stone walls, sluices and channels, forming old sheepwash pens (Wp.26). The track runs along the eastern bank of the river, a path coming in across a bridge to the left (Wp.27). A verse from Wordsworth is carved into the bridge parapet, another parish marker: "Still glides the stream and shall forever glide, the form remains the function never dies". Not his best, I think.

The track leads us down the dale (NE) past a series of dams and fish breeding ponds where we cross a slab bridge across the river (Wp.28 270M). A lane leads up the hill to **Youlgrave** and the white house on the left is a tea shop - a welcome sight! After refreshments we go through a squeeze stile and walk along the northern bank of the river along a popular Sunday stroll route. We emerge by a few houses (Wp.29) where we cross a lane and continue ahead through a wicket gate by a farm gate misleadingly signed 'Haddon Estate, Private Road' (it is a public footpath). The track crosses the stream and passes by a bench under a rock overhang opposite a packhorse bridge. We follow the track alongside the river until it heads off right, the footpath continuing straight ahead through a squeeze stile along the dale and past the rock outcrop of **Rhienstor**. The path crosses the river, goes through a gate, and brings us back to the red telephone box at **Alport** (Wp.1 300M).

17 TADDINGTON & CHELMORTON: Ancient Landscapes & a Hill of Secrets

Two of the Peak District's most genuine, yet least known, villages feature in this walk. **Taddington** is bypassed by the A6, a rare blessing in the Peak District, and so is ignored by many visitors: a pity, because this is a 'real' village and a good centre for walking. The strip fields of **Chelmorton** reflect farming before the 18th century enclosures, while relics of lead mining on the hills above the village, and modern stone-trucks parked outside village houses, remind us that agriculture and mineral extraction remain the dual foundations of the traditional Peak District economy.

Evidence of human occupation far predating the enclosures is visible on these hills. Tumuli and burial chambers at **Chelmorton Low** and **Five Wells** date from the Bronze Age; north of the A6 near **Taddington**, the ancient landscape of **Priestcliffe** has cultivation terraces that represent some of mankind's earliest efforts at farming.

The villages are separated by the distinctive ridge visible to the south of the A6, formed by an ancient lava flow ejected from a volcano in the tropical Carboniferous sea 325 million years ago at **Calton Hill**, now visible as a rounded hill near the junction of the A6 and A5270. But it's not all it seems - what you see today is completely man made. The hard dolerite rock of the ancient volcano was quarried away for roadstone before the 1970s, leaving a gash in the landscape. The County Council restored the hill's slopes to their original shape with quarry waste leaving a hollow in the centre, winning the Council a conservation award in 1979. Landfilled for thirty years with refuse from **Buxton** and the **High Peak**, the hollow was completely filled by 2003. The final restoration will soon be complete, and the hill left to its secrets.

We finish at the sympathetically restored **High Well** at **Taddington**.

Without the lava flow, the villages would not be here: its impermeability to water forces percolating water out of the limestone at springs such as the one that feeds this well, providing a plentiful source of water in an otherwise waterless place where piped water arrived only a generation ago.

Safety Advice: 1. The stone stiles are very slippery when wet. 2. Take extreme care crossing the A6 with its lethal combination of lumbering stone trucks and high speed motorcyclists. 3. Take care in areas of lead workings - possibility of uncapped shafts.

Access by bus: TransPeak (**Buxton** to **Bakewell**, frequent) to bus stop at the upper end of **Taddington**.

Access by car: A6 to **Taddington**. Park unobstructively on street near the turning for **Flagg**.

> **Alternative start/finish** **Chelmorton** (limited parking).

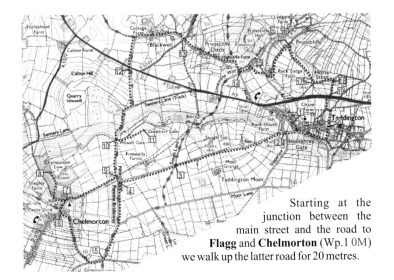

Starting at the junction between the main street and the road to **Flagg** and **Chelmorton** (Wp.1 0M) we walk up the latter road for 20 metres.

Just past a house name sign 'Daybreak Cottage' on the right, we take a narrow path by a cypress hedge and head uphill (W) through three stiles, across another lane (Wp.2) and on uphill (WSW), enjoying views back over **Taddington** village towards the distinctive cultivation terraces of **Priestcliffe** and towards **Wyedale** and **Longstone Edge**. The path continues across a number of derelict walls to the top of **Sough Top** hill, topped with mobile phone masts and a covered reservoir. The hill's name refers to a lead mine drainage tunnel, the 'Waterloo Sough', cut under the hill from near **The Waterloo** pub on the A6.

We cross a stone stile by the reservoir and continue west south-west for 800 metres with a wall on our right, and cross seven stone stiles, then crossing a track at Wp.3 (30M). On the same heading for another 700 metres, we cross another five stone stiles with **Fivewells Farm** on our right, to reach **Pilwell Lane** at Wp.4 (for a shorter walk, missing **Chelmorton**, Wp.9 is only 100 metres north). Here we turn left and follow the lane south for 900 metres, bearing right where it joins a larger lane, to reach a crossroads at Wp.5 (50M). We turn right and follow **Flagg Lane** (careful, it's a rat-run) for 200 metres to a junction where we take the lane on the right to **Chelmorton**.

Chelmorton and its dry stone walls

As we round the hill **Chelmorton** village and its stone walls preserving the pre-Enclosures strip field pattern come into view. In much of England, the Enclosures were an excuse for a land-grab by the rich and powerful, obliterating the historical field patterns along with the peasantry, but here the original fields were enclosed. Maintenance of these stone walls is a priority for the National Park.

The Church Inn

In the village we turn right at a T-junction (Wp.6 60M) to pass the church and **The Church Inn** (food served). Clever name - local drinkers could tell their families, "I'm off to The Church" and go to the pub, without telling a porkie! The road ends past the pub and we turn left (Wp.7) to climb **Chelmorton Low** through a gate on the left (this bit is optional).

The slopes of **Chelmorton Low**, but not the enclosed fields, are Right to Roam land. We follow the muddy bridleway alongside the wall (NW), past a grassy mound (old lead workings), then strike out uphill. Around halfway up we meet and follow a derelict wall before heading for the hilltop with its two large neolithic burial mounds, and views over **Chelmorton** and towards **Buxton** and **High Peak** (Wp.8 75M).

Retracing our steps to Wp.7, we turn left, passing a spring in woods on the left, the source of the **Illy Willy Water**, historically **Chelmorton's** water supply. The path climbs on an embankment beside a hollow area on the left, then runs through a hummocky area, along which we take the northernmost (left hand) path. These are all evidence of lead workings: two *rakes* or vertical veins converged here, mined both in pits from the surface and from underground mines. Keep to the paths as there may be old uncapped shafts amongst the hummocks - no-one knows where all the old shafts were.

On reaching **Pilwell Lane** (Wp.9 95M) we follow it north between stone walls (ignore the track to the farm) to the top of the ridge. Just before **Pilwell Gate** (Wp.10) a footpath sign on the right marks a concession path to **Five Wells Cairn**.

The Neolithic chambered cairn

We follow this (this bit's optional too) across two fields to and through a stone stile on the right to reach the Neolithic chambered cairn (Wp.11 110M), a form of burial mound, built at a vantage point overlooking the countryside to the north. **Tunstead Quarry** to the north-west, the largest in Europe, is noted for the purity of its limestone, while below is the mineral railway running through **Great Rocks Dale** - named of course by the quarry's Marketing Department.

Returning to **Pilwell Gate**, we continue north and descend the scarp slope past Heath Robinson-style black painted smallholding buildings; the line of rock outcropping along the face of the slope is the top of the lava flow. The rounded

Calton Hill (the former volcano) is to our left. We come to a tarmac road by a security gate, the entrance to the former landfill site, with a compound containing equipment to treat methane gas and polluted water from the waste: ugly, but essential protection of the environment. We head almost due north down the tarmac to the A6 (Wp.12 135M: bus stop).

Before crossing, it's worth looking back up to **Calton Hill**, which from here looks entirely natural. We cross the A6 with extreme care and follow the lane opposite, almost due north, then curving past a caravan site and through the small hamlet of **Blackwell** to a crossroads with the B6049 (Wp.13 150M). Crossing the road, we continue up the lane on the opposite side through the hamlet of **Priestcliffe Ditch**, up the hill and round the corner at the top to **Priestcliffe** crossroads (Wp.14 165M) where we turn left along **Priestcliffe Lane**. We take a footpath across a field on the right, just before the front drive to a house, to reach another lane opposite **Rock Lodge Farm** (Wp.15); we turn right then left into the farmyard, then left at a footpath sign past the house, and north-east along an overgrown path between stone walls and past farm buildings. Just after a wooden barn on the right (Wp.16 180M) we take the waymarked footpath on the right around the foot of the hill.

Passing through several stone stiles, we cross cultivation terraces on the hillside, and at the top of the rise, before reaching the A6, take a small green lane on the left (Wp.7). Crossing a field below a small copse, we turn right (almost back on ourselves) through a squeeze stile, then follow the path (S) to reach the A6 Taddington Bypass dual carriageway (Wp.18 195M). Take care crossing - this is the only overtaking opportunity for motorists between **Buxton** and **Matlock**, so they go for it. Steps on the opposite side on the right lead us to a stile; we head south, reaching a track where we turn left, then right on another path heading due south, leading us to **Taddington's** village street.

High Well

A short detour to the left would lead us to refreshments at **The Queen's Arms** pub, but to complete the walk we continue straight ahead on a path opposite. The path zigzags left, right and left again by a green sign, up the hill to and past a sheltered seat to reach **High Well**, which formed where a fault line displaced the limestone and the lava flow, allowing water to spring out of the ground ; it's been sympathetically restored. Note particularly how the cattle watering pond is outside the walled enclosure, to keep the source pure - the same arrangement I've seen at village wells across Africa, from Baidoa in Somalia to Malawi. This is a fine viewpoint and picnic area.

Leaving **High Well**, we retrace our steps past the shelter but instead of zigzagging back down the hill at the green sign, we keep straight ahead and follow a path west that contours along the hillside past a number of cottages - some surprisingly derelict in this desirable area - leading us to a road by a '30' sign. Following this road downhill brings us back to our starting point (Wp.1 210M).

18 ROOKERY & MAGPIE:
Wealth Beneath Our Feet

Today the countryside south of **Wyedale**, between **Ashford in the Water** and **Sheldon**, presents an impression of rural serenity disturbed only by modern traffic on the A6. But it wasn't always so; in bygone centuries, even in living memory, the area would have rung to the sounds of miner' picks and hammers and been shaken by the explosions of rock blasting. The wealth between the ground included lead, mined from several *rakes* (veins), fluorspar (briefly important as lead mining declined), and several varieties of ornamental marble. All these are gone now, and their traces can be hard to find. The exception is **Magpie Lead Mine**, at which ruined buildings preserved by the Peak District Mines Historical Society majestically dominate the plateau. Lead mining has taken place here since at least 1674. Mechanical pumping was introduced in the 1820s following a strike of rich ore in 1810.

Chasing this ore, the Magpie miners broke into workings from the neighbouring **Redsoil Mine**, starting a dispute that was to have tragic consequences. Derbyshire's unique *Barmote Laws* governed lead mining and were usually well able to resolve such disputes, granting miners who successfully extracted ore from a vein exclusive rights to a given length of that vein. It wasn't possible to tell apart the many veins in this location, however, and the dispute continued to fester; the miners resorted to violence, and each side attempted to smoke the others out by setting underground fires of straw and highly toxic tar culminating in 1833 with the asphyxiation by fumes of three Redsoil miners and the trial, and later acquittal, of the Magpie miners for murder. Unsurprisingly, bitterness persisted well into living memory in **Sheldon** between their descendants. The existing buildings date from the latter part of the 1800s when Cornish mining expertise and equipment were brought in to work the mine to deeper levels. Despite the eight year struggle (1873 to 1881) to blast the 2 kilometre long **Magpie Sough** tunnel, draining the mine to the **River Wye**, these later attempts to work the mine remained barely profitable. It closed for the last time in the 1950s.

This walk has more than industrial history to commend it. We pass through deciduous woodlands rich in birdlife, over grassland rich in cowslips and orchids, and through the unique habitat of old lead workings, where contamination of the soil means that only metal tolerant plants such as Leadwort will grow. We follow the **River Wye** and visit the attractive village of **Ashford in the Water** with its medieval **Sheepwash Bridge**, and **Sheldon**.

We start and finish in **Ashford in the Water**, an attractive village with good facilities west of **Bakewell**, bypassed by the A6. We pass the sites of marble quarries and mines and ascend to the plateau level near **Sheldon**, where we explore the area of **Magpie Mine**. After refreshments in **Sheldon**, we head for a viewpoint over **Deep Dale**, then descend across access land to the reputedly haunted **Dimin Dale**, returning along **Wyedale**, through **Great Shacklow Wood**, past the outfall of the **Magpie Sough**, finally to **Ashford** across **Sheepwash Bridge**.

3   3½ H   7½ miles/12km   320m / 320m   3

Safety Advice: 1. Extreme care required crossing the A6. 2. Take care near lead and marble workings - possibility of uncapped shafts; do not enter mine workings. 3. Wash hands before eating after coming into contact with soil near old lead mines.

Access by bus: TransPeak (**Buxton - Bakewell**, frequent) and N°173 (**Bakewell - Tideswell**, 2 hourly, daily) to **Ashford**. Alight at **Ashford Arms** (Wp.20).

Access by car: Turn off the A6 to **Ashford**: park in the small car park near the toilets or unobstructively on street.

> **Alternative start/finish**
> **White Lodge** car park, by the A6 near **Dimin Dale** (Wp.16); **Sheldon** (Wp.11).

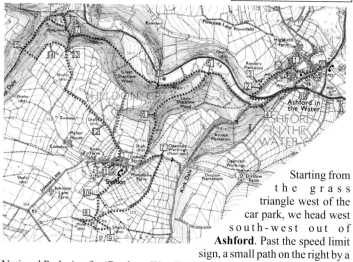

Starting from the grass triangle west of the car park, we head west south-west out of **Ashford**. Past the speed limit sign, a small path on the right by a National Park sign for 'Rookery Wood' (Wp.2 4M) rises into the wood past a wooden fence; we follow it for around 50 metres, then fork sharp right, still climbing. Following yellow and orange arrows fixed to trees, we branch to the left and come to the grilled mine entrance to **Rookery Mine** at the back of an old quarry face (Wp.3 12M) from where ornamental black marble (fine examples can be seen in **Chatsworth House**) was hewn. Retracing our steps to the road, we can see that the woodland has naturally regenerated an area of intensive quarrying and spoil tipping.

Continuing along the road, we come to the A6 and cross with extreme care. On the far side of the road is a National Park Authority yard, originally the marble mill where the stone was cut and polished. We head east for 100 metres along the footpath beside the A6, over the **River Wye**, then turn right (SW) along a lane, passing an old quarry on the left where further black marble mines were located (**Arrock Mine**, no access; Wp.4 20M). After 200 metres our footpath diverges right, through a gate and takes a north-westerly direction alongside the **River Wye**, until the path curves left to pass through another gate (Wp.5 30M). Here we turn left and head along the side valley of **Nettler Dale** (SE) into **Little Shacklow Wood**. The path rises along the bottom of the dale, passing a small conifer plantation before the dale divides into two.

Our footpath follows the left hand valley, heading south. Old quarry workings on both sides of the path, now moss covered, are remnants of further marble mines. Past the spoil tips (Wp.6 48M), a faint path on the left leads to the cavernous entrance of the **Bird's Eye Marble Mine** (a source of a form of black marble with Crinoid fossils) - now dangerously unstable and not to be entered.

Returning to the path, we continue up the dale, past other marble workings, leaving the wood at a gate, continuing along the dale, past the old sewage works to a lane, where we turn left, following it uphill. At the hilltop our path follows a track to the right (Wp.7 65M). The fields on the north side of the lane are not what they seem; in the 1960s and 70s these were the deep opencast workings for fluorspar of **Dirtlow Rake**, now restored.

We follow the track with views of Sheldon to the west, to its end at a stile, with the **Magpie Mine** buildings ahead, then follow the waymarked footpath towards the mine. Crossing the last stile before the mine, we pass the old reservoir, now dry, and a roofless circular building - the gunpowder store, well away from the mine buildings, before reaching the round chimney beside the tall engine house (Wp.8 90M).

The replica of the *whim*

By two millstones (originally used to crush ore) we head east south-east to the wooden structure visible across the hummocky ground of the old lead spoil. This is a replica, constructed at the site of the **Redsoil Mine**, of the original horse-driven *whim* or winding gear that would have been found on hundreds of small lead mines across the Peak District (Wp.9 94M).

Wandering round, you'll find several old shafts, now carefully covered with grilles. The thousands of old shafts dotted around the lead mining areas are by no means all recorded or safely capped: Derbyshire County Council has to employ an engineer full time to make old mine workings safe.

The hummocks are more sparsely vegetated than the surrounding fields: this is *Belland Ground*, land contaminated by lead from the mines. Short term, one-off visitors should not be exposed to harmful amounts, but do wash your hands before eating, just in case! In spring the ground is dusted white by the small flowers of the Leadwort or Spring Sandwort, an unusually metal-resistant plant.

Leaving the *whim*, we head directly towards the cottage (E) on the south side of the mine buildings, and after crossing a track and mounting a hummock we reach **Crossvein Shaft**, where the circular path plodded by ponies operating the winding gear can still be seen. At the cottage (originally the mine agent's house), there are good views of the mine's headworks. The corrugated iron sheds and the metal headstocks, dating from the last attempt to work the mine in the 1950s, are still used by the Mines Historical Society to access the mine.

The mine's remains

The stone buildings, including the chimneys, the wooden winding wheel and the tall engine house, date from 1840 to 1870 when industrial scale mining was introduced. Apart from some old shafts, nothing remains of the two centuries of mining that went before.

From the cottage we loop west of the old mine buildings, passing the **Shuttlebark Engine Shaft** by the footpath sign at the west end of the site, taking a look at the modern headstocks, then returning to the round chimney (Wp.8) through the area where ore crushing and washing used to take place. Taking our leave of the mine, we head north through a stile, and cross a flat field heading towards **Sheldon**. At a junction of paths (Wp.10 110M) we fork right to head north-west along the valley, then turn left when we reach the lane in **Sheldon** village, bringing us to **The Cock and Pullet Inn** (Wp.11 120M), a welcome opportunity to partake of food and excellent beer.

From the pub, we retrace our steps for a few yards, then take a small lane north past the chapel and across fields. Shortly after ignoring a footpath on the right (an alternative shorter descent to **Great Shacklow Wood**), we leave this track on the left by a field path, heading north-west. Much evidence of lead mining is visible; we're following the line of the **Fieldgrove Vein**, crossing several stiles until a track comes in from the left and the path turns sharp right (NE) with a wall on our left. On reaching a stile in this wall we head north north-west diagonally across the field to another stile where we enter the access land of the **Deep Dale** nature reserve (Wp.13 135M).

To shorten the walk you could continue down the steep path, reaching Wp.17 in 5 minutes: but the longer route described is worth the extra effort. To follow this route we turn left to follow the wall uphill, to reach a small knoll (Wp.14 150M). There are fine views over the **Wye Valley**, towards the woods of **Monsal** and **Taddington Dales** and the high ground of **Fin Cop** to the north, with **Deep Dale** to the south-west. We head in the latter direction along the rim of **Deep Dale** through grassland rich in wild flowers and orchids in spring and summer. When we reach a gully (formed by surface lead workings in a vein) crossing our path we follow it carefully, to the foot of the dale (Wp.15 160M) where we turn right.

We follow the path along the foot of the dale until it bears right through a rocky defile, emerging on a natural terrace, the site of a prehistoric settlement. Although nothing is visible now, it's easy to see why this easily defended area with its natural ramparts of limestone outcrops was an attractive settlement site. At the junction of paths (Wp.16 164M) we bear right, but first take a short there-and-back detour left to view the rocky mouth of the reputedly haunted **Dimin Dale** (N.B. This path leads to the **White Lodge** car park on the A6).

Our path slopes steeply up to a gate at another path junction (Wp.17 172M) where we follow the path for **Ashford** into **Great Shacklow Wood** along a narrow terrace through the woods, high above the **Wye Valley**, before descending to the edge of the wood. Ignoring a path crossing, we continue along the edge of the wood until reaching a fast flowing stream entering the **River Wye**; no natural spring, but the man-made tunnel of **Magpie Sough**, blasted between 1873 and 1881 to drain the **Magpie Mine** (Wp.18 205M).

The *sough* was used at one time as an underground canal to bring calcite out of the mine. During the 1950s it was reputedly used by some miners to slip out of the 'back door' of the mine and walk into **Ashford** for lunch and a few beers at **The Ashford Arms**; we follow their route for the remainder of the walk, so we can work out how little time they must have spent actually mining. Small wonder the mine made no profit! Despite the fact that it drains a lead mine, the water is of high purity (lead is quite insoluble) and makes an important contribution to the flow of the **River Wye**.

Shortly after passing the *sough*, we reach the old **Shacklow Mill**, formerly used for a range of industrial purposes including crushing the mineral Barite, making bobbins for cotton spinning and crushing scrap tin cans. Before reaching the mill, note the waterwheel on the left, below a metal tripod and with two pipes crossing the *launder*. This originally powered the compressors for the rock drills that tunnelled the *sough*, and was then converted to pump water up to **Sheldon** after its wells dried up when the *sough* lowered the water table.

Sheepwash Bridge

Continuing along the south bank of the **River Wye**, we rejoin our outward route at the foot of **Nettler Dale** and retrace our steps past **Arrock Mine** to the A6. Bearing right, we follow the footpath alongside the trunk road for 200 metres until on the opposite side we see **Sheepwash Bridge** (Wp.19 232M).

With extreme care we cross the A6 and, after taking in this classic view of the bridge, we cross over it and turn right into **Ashford**. Passing the church, **The Bull's Head** and the village shop on our left, we continue along the street to arrive at **The Ashford Arms** (Wp.20 236M). Formerly the Devonshire Arms, this pub was where the *Barmote Court* for the Ashford Liberty was held, to administer the lead mining laws and adjudicate the many disputes involving the **Magpie Mine**. To return to our start, we retrace our steps towards the church, then take **Court Lane** on the right, passing behind the church to our starting point (Wp.1 240M).

19 LITTON, CRESSBROOK DALE, PETER'S STONE & ASHFORD

Of all the attractive side dales that run into **Wyedale**, **Cressbrook Dale** is one of the most appealing. From the dry valley cut into the plateau at the north end, to the wooded ravine of the southern end, it provides a range of natural habitats. The dale is managed as a nature reserve by English Nature.

The upper part of **Cressbrook Dale** is dominated by the large rock of **Peter's Stone**, said to resemble St Peter's Basilica in the Vatican City; hmmm. It's a landslipped mass of limestone rock that slid on a weak clayey layer of weathered volcanic ash in the limestone. The walk allows us to ascend this lofty eyrie before descending along the dale to **Cressbrook Mill**, along **Monsal Dale** to **Monsal Head**, then passing across meadowland on the eastern shoulder of **Fin Cop** to return to **Ashford**.

This walk is best done by parking at **Ashford in the Water**, taking the scenic Hulleys N°173 bus service from **Ashford** through the **Longstones** and **Monsal Head** to **Litton**, and walking back to **Ashford**, mainly downhill. For those wanting a bit more edge, combine it with the ascent of **Fin Cop** described in Walk 20.

1 | 1H 50M | 7½ miles/12km | 160m | 330m | * | 2

* bus out, walk back

Safety Advice: 1. Do not attempt the ascent of **Fin Cop** in hill fog: both the ascent and descent are on unclear paths with cliffs and crags close by.

Access by bus: N°173 **Bakewell-Tideswell** (2 hourly, 7 days/week) to **Ashford** and **Litton**.

Access by car: Turn off the A6 to **Ashford in the Water**. Park in the small car park near the toilets or unobstructively on street.

Alternative start
Monsal Head; **Litton**.

If parking in **Ashford** and taking the bus to **Litton**, we make our way to the eastern end of the village, past **The Ashford Arms** and ignoring the bus stops there, to the T-junction with the A6020. Turning left, we come to the **Ashford New Road** bus stop opposite the cricket pavilion, where we pick up the N°173 bus in the direction of **Tideswell**. We alight in **Litton** by the red phone box on the village green (Wp.1) where the walk starts. Refreshments can be had at **The Red Lion**, just behind the stocks on the village green; the **Litton** village shop is by the bus stop.

From the phone box we walk east along the village street past a chapel and a farm, and take the signposted footpath over a stile on the right (Wp.2 4M) diagonally across a field to a stile. The path joins a track and we go left and then right across another stile (Wp.3 7M), crossing more pastureland to enter the nature reserve, and access land, at the head of **Tansley Dale** (Wp.4 10M). Two routes are signed; the public footpath descends into the dale but we take the left fork, a concession path running beside a wall along the rim of the dale. Evidence of lead mining abounds - shafts, grassed over tailings ponds - and this path offers views over **Tansley Dale** and later, **Cressbrook Dale**. After passing a dewpond, we reach the lip of **Cressbrook Dale** where the path abruptly turns north, crosses a stile, and follows the wall along the rim of **Cressbrook Dale**, with a panoramic view of **Peter's Stone** opposite, eventually running parallel with **Mires Lane** to reach a gate by an English Nature signboard (Wp.5 30M).

Spring orchids

The signposted footpath runs alongside the wall, but we head to its right to walk above a line of small crags on a gentle descent to the bottom of **Cressbrook Dale** through grassland rich with cowslips, primroses and orchids in spring, and with **Peter's Stone** prominent to the south. A wall runs along the foot of

Peter's Stone

the dale but it has fallen in places, and taking care not to damage the surviving sections, we cross through a gap onto the footpath on the far side (Wp.6 37M). Turning right, we come shortly to a fork where we take the concession path signed on the left to **Peter's Stone** up around the stone's western side; its top seems impregnable at first, but a scramble to it is possible via a fissure on the west side (Wp.7 45M).

From the stone we descend to the valley floor, either heading a short distance south then directly west down the slope (taking care to avoid crags), or by retracing steps along the concession path. At the bottom we turn left and head down the grassy dale which may, depending on groundwater levels, be dry or have a stream running. Passing the stepping stones for the **Tansley Dale** path, we keep to the path in the bottom of **Cressbrook Dale**, ignoring the footpath that runs up the hillside on the left to **Wardlow** (but note the old mine shaft in the middle of this path near the fork!).

As the dale bends right we enter a wooded area and remain in woodland for the next half mile or so, often muddy underfoot, but frequently enhanced by the white flowers of the Wood Anemone (*Anemone nemorosa*). Brushwood from thinning of the woodland has been left in piles along the path by English Nature to encourage insect life. Shortly after a path comes in from the left we cross a footbridge, then bear left to follow the dale bottom to **Ravensdale Cottages**, (see photo over page) a small street of terraced cottages dramatically located under **Ravencliffe Crags**.

Ravensdale Cottages

We continue south along the lane leading from the cottages - the bottom of the dale here is kept for wildlife - and ascend gently to a road junction (Wp.8 90M). Taking the footpath diagonally opposite, we ascend to a lane by houses where we bear left to reach a road junction by a gatehouse with a white fence at the private entrance to **Cressbrook Hall** (Wp.9 100M). Turning left, we head down the lane with occasional views of **Water Cum Jolly Dale** on the right, and after another lane comes in from the left we reach the junction with the path through **Cressbrook Mill** (Wp.10 110M).

A short detour to the right brings us to **Cressbrook Millpond** in **Water cum Jolly Dale**, and (at weekends) **D's Brew Stop**, a somewhat alternative tea shop (bring your own food!) gloriously at odds with the executive ambience of today's **Cressbrook**. Suitably refreshed, we return to Wp.10 and turn right to continue along the lane past the mill entrance, then running alongside the meadows in the base of **Monsal Dale**.

The footbridge over the River Wye

We pass through the hamlet of **Upperdale** and continue through this pastoral scene until, with **Monsal Head** in view and the lane about to climb out of the valley, we take a bridleway diverging right towards a farm. Just before the farm (Wp.11 125M) we take the signposted footpath on the right to cross the footbridge over the **River Wye**, then bear left to pass under the **Monsal Dale** viaduct.

(To shorten the walk, take the second path on the right up to the viaduct, then cross it and ascend to **Monsal Dale**).

Passing through a stile by a gate, the path continues south-west along the flat riverside pasture, with views of the **Hobs House** landslip and **Fin Cop** on the far side of the dale, and then through an attractive wooded area. The noise of rushing water alerts us to the **Monsal Dale Weir**, which we pass by, soon reaching and crossing a footbridge (Wp.12 150M). Now the path starts to return towards **Monsal Head**. When the fence on the right ends, a steep unmarked path climbs steeply up the bank, the route to **Hobs House** and **Fin Cop** described in Walk 20. However our route follows the main path through the woods, ascending gently to **Monsal Head**, where both pub and tea shop offer refreshments (Wp.13 165M).

Just before reaching the lane at the top of the rise, you'll have noticed a footpath signposted 'Ashford' heading south-west along the rim of the dale. Suitably refreshed, we follow this path through a gate, then alongside the wall running along the rim, eventually passing through a wicket gate on the left

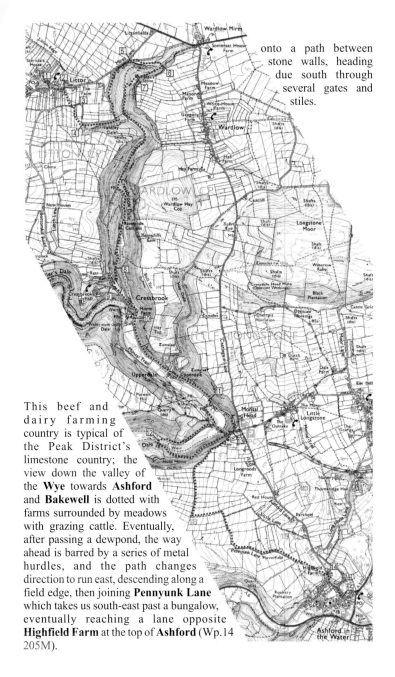

onto a path between stone walls, heading due south through several gates and stiles.

This beef and dairy farming country is typical of the Peak District's limestone country; the view down the valley of the **Wye** towards **Ashford** and **Bakewell** is dotted with farms surrounded by meadows with grazing cattle. Eventually, after passing a dewpond, the way ahead is barred by a series of metal hurdles, and the path changes direction to run east, descending along a field edge, then joining **Pennyunk Lane** which takes us south-east past a bungalow, eventually reaching a lane opposite **Highfield Farm** at the top of **Ashford** (Wp.14 205M).

Ignoring the cul-de-sac serving the houses on the right, we turn right on the main lane, then almost immediately left to descend along the steep street of **Hillcroft**, bearing right on meeting the B6465 to reach the end of our walk by the village grocer opposite **The Ashford Arms** (Wp.15 215M). Refreshments can be had here or at the nearby **Bull's Head**, before heading home.

20 FIN COP & HOBS HOUSE: Short & Sharp from Monsal Head

One of the best viewpoints in the Peak District, and a unique and dramatic rock formation - **Fin Cop** and **Hobs House** - lie just to the west of **Monsal Head**, but with no public footpath access, have remained off limits and virtually unknown to visitors. Right to Roam has changed this, but has not made access either easy or simple, for while the obvious route to the headland of **Fin Cop** would be along the ridge from **Monsal Head**, the designated access area does not include the woodland on the ridge. Whilst the summit is designated access land, access has therefore to be gained from the bottom of **Monsal Dale** - near the footbridge by the weir - by climbing the steep north facing slope.

The jumbled rocks of the **Hobs House** landslip have to be negotiated first. A weak and slippery layer of weathered lava has caused these huge limestone rocks to slide down from the face of **Fin Cop**, taking a bite out of the hillside and leaving a jumble of boulders, rocks and crevasses below, blocking the obvious route to the top of **Fin Cop**.

This walk is described as a short but sharp circular from **Monsal Head**, but those looking for a longer walk can combine it with linear Walk 19 from **Litton** to **Ashford**.

| 4 | 1H 50M | 3 miles/5km | 260m / 260m | ↻ | 2 |

Safety Advice: 1. Do not attempt ascent of **Fin Cop** in hill fog, as the ascent and descent is on unclear paths with cliffs and crags close by.

Access by bus: N°173 **Bakewell-Tideswell** to **Monsal Head**.

> **Alternative start**
> **White Lodge** car park, by the A6 at **Lees Bottom**; follow the footpath up **Monsal Dale** to the footbridge (Wp.3).

Access by car: B6465 from **Ashford** to **Monsal Head.** Park in pay car park.

Starting at the crossroads at **Monsal Head** (Wp.1) we follow the lane for **Cressbrook** west past the hotel to the viewpoint at the hairpin bend by the tea shop.

Monsal Dale Viaduct

We take the path to the right, signposted for the viaduct, but at the junction of paths where the viaduct path turns left, we continue straight ahead to descend into the dale. After passing a farm we turn left (Wp.2 7M) and cross the footbridge over the **River Wye**, then bear left to pass under the **Monsal Dale Viaduct**.

Passing through a stile by a gate, the path continues south-west along the flat riverside pasture and then through an attractive wooded area, enjoying extensive views of the **Hobs House** landslip and **Fin Cop**; the ascent appears fairly daunting from this side. The noise of rushing water alerts us to the **Monsal Dale Weir** which we pass by, coming shortly after to a footbridge (Wp.3 20M).

Monsal Dale Weir

Crossing the footbridge, the path starts turning back towards **Monsal Head**, but shortly, after the fence on the right ends, we turn right on to an unsigned path climbing steeply up the bank. The path, faint in places, heads towards the right of the **Hobs House** rocks, which soon come into view. We come to a short grassy ridge with sporadic hawthorn bushes where a rocky hollow behind the rocks leads off to the left (Wp.4 27M); we'll return here on our descent, but for now leave **Hobs House** to the hobgoblin that resides here, to find a route up the hillside.

... the primrose-covered hillside ...

Traversing to the right across a bed of moss-covered boulders, we come to a very faint path heading diagonally south-west on a steep course up the primrose-covered and orchid-dotted hillside (in spring). The path becomes fainter as we climb, taking care not to damage the flowers, but we persevere until the view up the straight **Deep Dale** opens up to the south.

The slope lessens slightly, and we change direction to head directly uphill (SE) to cross the old defensive earthwork. Heading east, we reach the crest of the ridge by the corner of a stone wall (Wp.5 50M), where we are rewarded by extensive views north, west and south, reaching as far as the gritstone moors above **Buxton**.

We are not yet at the summit of **Fin Cop** so we head due south along the wall, which rises gently to a cairn a few hundred yards on (Wp.6 60M). Now views open up to the east and south-east, to include **Ashford** and **Bakewell**, and the gritstone moors above **Chatsworth House**, whose hunting tower is visible to the east. This commanding summit was the site of a prehistoric hill settlement, its strategic defensible location an obvious choice.

Returning to the corner of the wall at Wp.5, we commence our descent (W), but at the old earthwork change direction to follow a faint path diagonally downhill (NE) towards the viaduct. As the path reaches the trees (Wp.7 70M) we are rewarded with a dramatic view of the **Hobs House** rocks from above. Now we have to change direction as the path we've been following becomes dangerously confused with the crags above the landslip. We traverse left in a west north-west direction, bringing us back to our upward path, now our descent route to return to Wp.3 (80M).

... distinctive rock features ...

From Wp.3 we bear right and head along the rocky hollow that gives access to the rear of the **Hobs House** rocks, and take a little time to view the distinctive rock features. Particularly noticeable are the bands and nodules of dark, glassy rock inter-layered with the limestone: this is *chert*, a form of flint, mined near **Bakewell** and used in the potteries of **Stoke on Trent** to glaze the ware.

At the far end of the hollow a faint path leads east, gently downhill, to meet the main footpath. Turning right, we follow this path through woods to return to **Monsal Head**, where both pub and tea shop offer refreshments (Wp.1 110M).

The **River Wye** cuts through the **White Peak** plateau from **Buxton** to join the **River Derwent** at **Rowsley**, forming the largest of the Peak District dales. As it flows eastward, its character changes, along with its names. Only the narrow dale between **Buxton** and **Topley Pike** is truly named 'Wyedale'; scarred by quarrying and the A6, this is an unpromising start. But between **Topley Pike** and **Cressbrook**, as **Chee Dale**, **Miller's Dale** and **Water Cum Jolly Dale**, it becomes a dramatic, rock-sided gorge before broadening out into the flat bottomed pastoral **Monsal Dale** as it curves round **Fin Cop** to meander past **Shacklow Woods**, **Ashford** and **Bakewell**.

Much of the dale is roadless - in places, so narrow that even the footpath along the river runs on stepping stones - but despite the difficult terrain the Midland Railway, finding other routes thwarted by landowners, drove the new **Derby** to **Manchester** railway (1863) through the dale via tunnels and viaducts. The short-sighted decision to close it in 1967 provided a bonus to walkers when the National Park took over the trackbed for use by walkers and cyclists. Now there are plans to re-lay and reopen the railway, providing rail travellers with access to the southern Peak District for the first time in a generation.

Wyedale is a microcosm of the whole of the southern Peak District: clear rivers, springs, caves, limestone crags, drystone walls, pastureland; beef and dairy farming, lead mining, quarrying, lime burning, cotton mills; all were here, and their stories are amply retold by the multitude of signboards along the old railway trackbed. Much has returned to nature, turning the dale into a haven for rare plants and wildlife, managed as a nature reserve.

Litton and **Cressbrook** mills remain, famous for their use of child labour from London's poorhouses, but their conversion into yuppie-style apartments, whilst preserving the fine buildings, has inevitably ripped out their industrial hearts. All references to **Cressbrook Mill's** industrial past have been obliterated, and it now resembles a faux stately home. At **Litton Mill** where once Ellis Needham's child workers toiled for 16 hour days, garden-centre model badgers with wheelbarrows now ornament the windows. Doubtless the old poseur Ruskin, who complained about the railway, would have approved.

This circular walk (including a 'new' Right to Roam section) starts from **Monsal Head**, though the old station at **Miller's Dale Junction** serves equally well as a start. In full it's a long walk, though lots of shorter options make use of several well-marked footpaths that converge on **Priestcliffe** from between **Miller's Dale** and **Litton Mill**. Linear walks can be done by use of the TransPeak TP bus service along the A6 between Ashford and Topley Pike, the N°173 service between Ashford and Tideswell and the N°s 65 & 66 services between **Buxton**, **Sheffield** and **Chesterfield** via **Miller's Dale**.

Two points to note: the Right to Roam section on the ridge between **Cressbrook** and **Priestcliffe Lees** involves the negotiation of three new fences without stiles despite the access land designation. With care it can be done, but for those with dogs or who dislike climbing fences, there's an alternative path at lower level. The **Chee Dale** section from **Topley Pike** to **Wormhill Springs**, where the path uses stepping stones in the river, is impassable when the river is in flood, and rough and slippery at other times; the alternative footpath passes through **Blackwell Hall**.

Safety Advice: 1. The section through **Chee Dale** is slippery and prone to flooding. 2. Take care in areas of lead workings - possibility of uncapped shafts.

Alternative start/finish
Miller's Dale; **Topley Pike**; **Taddington**.

Access by bus: N°173 **Bakewell-Tideswell** to **Monsal Head**; TransPeak (**Buxton-Bakewell**, frequent) to **Taddington** and **Blackwell Turn**; N°s.65/66 **Buxton-Tideswell** to **Miller's Dale**.

Access by car: B6465 from **Ashford** to **Monsal Head**; B6049 from **Tideswell** to **Miller's Dale**; A6 to **Topley Pike**: park in pay car parks (beware of car crime, particularly at **Topley Pike**).

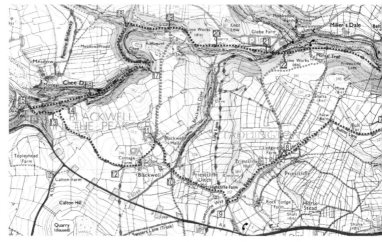

Monsal Dale Viaduct

Starting at the crossroads at **Monsal Head** (Wp.1) we follow the lane for **Cressbrook** past the hotel (W) to the viewpoint at the hairpin bend by the tea shop, and admire the view of **Monsal Vale Viaduct** crossing the dale. Following the directions on the sign, we turn right for the viaduct which seems wrong at first, but we soon reach a junction of paths (Wp.2 3M) where we turn left to descend to the viaduct by a blocked tunnel entrance.

Crossing the viaduct (check if the river is in flood, for later) we follow the **Monsal Trail** along the trackbed north-west, noting old lead workings at a calcite-filled vein left, the old **Monsal Dale Station** and the view of

Cressbrook Mill right.

After about a mile the footpath leaves the trackbed before another blocked tunnel. After passing through the gate on the right (Wp.3 25M) the path forks and we take the smaller, left fork and leave the main path, climbing through scrub with **Cressbrook Mill** visible on the right. Re-emerging into grassland on a ridge, we enjoy views of the Victorian **Cressbrook Hall** and houses on the high ground opposite. On reaching the nose of the ridge we leave the path and take a route directly uphill along it. (Note: to avoid negotiating fences, continue on this path, which rejoins the old railway near **Litton Mill**, then take the footpath uphill from the bridge at Wp.23 to rejoin the main walk at Wp.6 above **Priestcliffe Lees**.)

Magnificent views over the mill dam in **Water Cum Jolly Dale**, backed by the **Rubicon Wall** rockface (who came up with these names?) and the crags of **Ravenscliff** overlooking **Cressbrook Dale**, reward us for this steep ascent. Looking upriver, it's clear that the rocky gorge has been cut down below the bottom of an older valley, the result of the destructive power of snowmelt torrents during the Ice Ages.

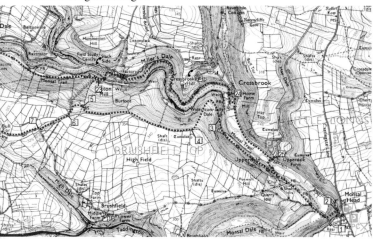

As we reach the wall at the top of the ridge by two hawthorns (Wp.4 45M), the view opens up across the plateau, and glimpses of **Kinder Scout** are revealed. Taking care around the old lead mine workings nearby, we turn right and head along the rim of the dale, soon coming to the first of the new fences. These can be crossed with the help of the bracing timbers for the corner posts, and we continue along the rim of the dale until reaching the third fence. Here we descend north to a dogleg in the fence, where we can cross at a corner post (Wp.5 70M) by some old lead mines, and follow a faint track west to join the footpath ascending from **Litton Mill** at a stile (Wp.6 75M).

We take the track (WSW) through an area of hummocky old lead workings, passing a sign for the 'Priestcliffe Lees Nature Reserve' by a gate (Wp.7 79M). Ignoring the track on the left, we continue straight ahead along a track, curving left by a barn to reach **Priestcliffe** farmstead (Wp.8 96M). Several paths from **Miller's Dale** converge on the farmstead from the right, offering shorter walking options - see map.). We take the right hand of two tarmac lanes at a fork heading south-west to **Priestcliffe Cross** (Wp.9 105M) where we turn right (alternatively, straight ahead for refreshments at **The Waterloo Inn** by the A6, or left for **Taddington**).

The road through **Priestcliffe Ditch** takes us over the B6049 (Wp.10 120M). One hundred metres after the crossroads we take the tarmac drive on the right to **Blackwell Hall**. Just before reaching the farm buildings, a footpath sign (easily missed) offers two options (Wp.11 127M). The alternative route, avoiding the rough and possibly flooded **Chee Dale**, runs due north through the blue gateposts ahead: but our route runs left (S) through a stone stile, then south-west across a series of fields to rejoin the lane in **Blackwell**, where we turn right to head past a caravan site to a left-hand bend in the road (Wp.12 135M; the lane on the left leads to the Blackwell Turn bus stop on the A6).

We bear right and follow the **Pennine Bridleway** (NW), the restored slopes of **Calton Hill** on the left and the **Buxton Limeworks** in **Tunstead Quarry** ahead, the largest in Western Europe. After two gates the bridleway runs across an open field. About halfway across we bear right off the track to cross a stone stile to the left of a gate in the wall below us (the OS Explorer map is confusingly wrong here). We cross the field, following the wall on our left to a squeeze stile, then cross the corner of the next field to a wicket gate at the lip of **Chee Dale** (Wp.13 150M).

From here, a brief deviation right along the rim - not for vertigo sufferers - leads to the tops of several buttresses with commanding views over **Chee Dale** and **Great Rocks Dale**, including the rock climbers' favourite, **Plum Buttress** (Wp.14 155M).

Retracing our steps to the wicket gate, we zigzag down the steep path, turning right to rejoin the bridleway at a stile, and turning right again onto the **Monsal Trail** (Wp.15 170M; the path from **Topley Pike** joins here) flowers clinging to crevices in the deep rock cutting. The trackbed takes us above the **River Wye** (ENE), and is joined by another old trackbed (originally the main line to **Manchester**) before crossing the **River Wye** on a viaduct. The tunnel ahead emerges in **Chee Dale**, but instead, we take the footpath on the left just after the viaduct down steep slippery steps (Wp.16 180M) and back under it to join the narrow riverside path. We follow the river downstream to an overhanging rock cliff which we pass on stepping stones in the river, then to a footbridge where we ascend to a path junction (Wp.17 200M). The left fork for 'Miller's Dale' leads us under another viaduct and back across the river which now heads west, having turned through 180 degrees; we traverse more stepping stones before negotiating a rough, wet and slippery section with the river turning back to flow eastwards.

The path eventually climbs over rock steps and heads north into a side valley with a strongly flowing stream, heading for a footbridge (Wp.18 220M). The watercourse under the footbridge is dry; **Wormhill Springs** (caused by a series of faults and fissures in the limestone) can be seen boiling up out of the ground below it. In dry weather the water nearly doubles the flow in the **Wye**.

Wormhill Springs

From the springs, we continue beside the river (E) to reach a junction of paths by a footbridge; our alternative path from **Blackwell** emerges here (Wp.19 230M). As we continue, notice the dark brown rock with 'bubbles' beneath our feet, the **Lower Miller's Dale** basalt (locally called 'Toadstone') ejected as a lava flow from the volcano at **Calton Hill** 325 million years ago. Soon after, before a viaduct, a steep path on the left leads up onto the old railway trackbed which we follow east.

A large concrete structure on our left comes into view: the former **East Buxton** limekilns, now preserved. Peer inside the drawing tunnels at the base, where the quicklime was dug out, and take a short detour up a path beyond the kilns on the left (Wp.20 235M) to see the top of the kilns with the quarry tramlines still in place, and the large quarry, now returning to nature. A few minutes walk east brings us to the old **Miller's Dale Junction** station (Wp.21 240M), an alternative start to the walk with refreshments, car parking, and **The Angler's Rest** a short detour away in the bottom of the valley.

... one of a pair of high viaducts ...

From the platform's end we head south to pick up the **Monsal Trail**, then turn left to cross the valley on one of a pair of high viaducts. On the far side (Wp.22 243M) steps lead up to a large stone structure - another bank of limekilns, at the side of **Miller's Dale Quarry**.

You may be able to take a detour through the old quarry along concessionary paths, though these may be closed in spring. The quarry was active until the 1930s but has been so enthusiastically taken over by orchids, birds and butterflies that it is now a Site of Special Scientific Interest. The detour follows the footpath up towards **Priestcliffe**, then forks left along a concession path through the quarry floor, then left again on another public footpath to return to the old railway track. (If not open, follow the old railway track east towards **Litton Mill**.)

Look out for the rock climbing mecca of **Ravenstor Cliffs** in the valley below, and the interesting lava flow-front outcrop on the right in the cutting. Between here and Litton Mill, Several footpaths on the right climb out of the valley to converge on **Priestcliffe**, offering shorter alternatives to the main route.

Shortly after passing underneath a bridge (Wp.23 265M) our main path diverts left off the old railway and down to **Litton Mill**, across a footbridge. At the lane in the hamlet we turn right and go into the gates of **Litton Mill**, following the concession path to the left of the old mill buildings, now apartments.

The footpath continues as a pleasant amble along the bottom of the dale, following the curves of the river downstream, a favourite spot for coots, moorhens and even the elusive kingfisher.

The Rubicon Wall

The river widens out into the **Cressbrook** millpond, the sheer limestone crag of **Rubicon Wall** (probably festooned with rock climbers) on the left to reach a junction of paths across a small bridge (Wp.24 315M).

Cressbrook Mill

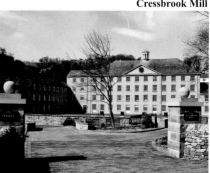

We turn left into **Cressbrook** and come to the folly, now **D's Brew Stop** (open at weekends), a splendidly alternative tea shop and essential antidote to the yuppification of **Cressbrook Mill**, ahead of us. After a brew we continue along the path by the iron railings past the mill, to emerge on a lane.

Turning right past the front gates of the mill, we head along the lane to the crossroads at the hamlet of **Upperdale** (Wp.25 330M) where we turn right, cross the river and ascend to pass under an old railway bridge. Just past the bridge we take the path left to regain the railway trackbed which we follow (SE).

We retrace our steps across **Monsal Head Viaduct**, then head back up the path to **Monsal Head**, where both pub and tea shop offer refreshments at the end of a long but interesting walk (Wp.1 345M).

As with **Dovedale** and the **Manifold Valley**, **Wyedale** can be explored as a linear walk, using the TransPeak (TP) bus service that runs along the A6. We park in **Ashford**, take the bus from **Ashford** to **Blackwell Turn** and walk back to **Ashford** using sections of Walk 21 and 19.

* bus out, walk back

Safety Advice: 1. The section through **Chee Dale** slippery and prone to flooding. 2. Care needed in crossing the A6.

Access by bus: TransPeak TP **Bakewell-Buxton** (2 hourly, 7 days/week) to **Ashford**, **Taddington** and **Blackwell Turn**.

> **Alternative start**
> **White Lodge** car park, by the A6 at foot of **Taddington Dale**; bus stop on A6 near the car park entrance.

Access by car: Turn off A6 to **Ashford**. Park in the small car park near the toilets, or unobstructively on the street.

If parking in **Ashford** and taking the bus to **Blackwell Turn**, make your way to the eastern end of the village, to the **Ashford Arms**. The bus stop on the same side of the road as the **Ashford Arms** is where we pick up the TP bus in the direction of **Buxton**. We alight at the bus stop by the road junction to Blackwell, carefully cross the A6 and take the lane opposite. Where the lane turns to the east, we are at Wp.12 of Walk 21.

You can follow either leg of Walk 21 to **Monsal Head**, but the timings and effort ratings above assume we turn left onto the bridleway and follow the return leg of Walk 21 through the dale, bringing us via **Chee Dale**, **Miller's Dale**, **Water Cum Jolly Dale** and **Monsal Dale** to the **Monsal Dale Viaduct** below **Monsal Head**.

Our route takes us up the path to **Monsal Head** - a good refreshment break - from where we follow the path signposted to **Ashford** described in Walk 19, from Wp.13 (the start of the **Ashford** path in **Monsal Head**) to the finish at the Ashford Arms at Wp.15. A slightly longer alternative from **Monsal Dale Viaduct** is to remain in the valley and return to **Ashford** via **White Lodge** car park and **Dimin Dale**, then follow Walk 18 through **Shacklow Woods**.

The Monsal Head Hotel

23 LONGSTONE EDGE & HIGH RAKE:
Green Grass, Purple Heather, Yellow Metal

The area of high ground to the north of the twin villages of **Great** and **Little Longstone** is one of the highest in the **White Peak** country and offers panoramic views in all directions, south towards **Bakewell**, west towards **Monsal Head**, **Fin Cop** and the high ground near **Buxton**, north towards **Mam Tor** and **Kinder Scout** and east towards **Chatsworth** and the gritstone of the **Derwent Edges**; a landscape of green grass and purple heather.

Whilst the distant views are attractive, the foreground views are challenging, for this is Fluorspar mining country, the successor to the now abandoned lead mining industry of the Peak District. Found in the same veins as lead, it was discarded as worthless *gangue* by the original lead miners, then came into demand as a flux when Sheffield's steelmakers changed to electric furnaces in the 1960s, and is now also used as a source of fluoride in a range of products, from toothpaste to electronics.

The modern opencast mines with the yellow metal of excavators, breakers, drills, crushers and powerscreens, their deep chasms and dusty white haul roads, may seem discordant in this environment, but they are the modern form of an indigenous industry that predates the National Park by 900 years, and helped create the Peak District's social fabric.

Within twenty years this industry will be gone, like the lead mining that came before it: the economic reserve of Fluorspar is running out and modern planning permissions are time limited. Restoration has already covered over the scars of many workings, and in years to come the restoration backfill will become a haven for rare limestone-loving wild flowers such as cowslips and orchids. Modern restoration techniques could completely obliterate all traces of mining; but a part of Peak District industrial history would be lost, together with the nesting sites already colonised by birds on the high artificial crags. I hope that one of the deep opencast pits can be left open, for posterity, and for nature to take back as it sees fit.

Safety Advice: 1. Take care near old lead workings - possibility of uncapped shafts. 2. Wash hands before eating after coming into contact with soil near old lead mines. 3. Obey signs and instructions near opencast mines, particularly about blasting. 4. Take care of lorries on haul roads during normal working hours.

Access by bus: N°173 **Bakewell-Tideswell** (2 hourly, 7 days/week) to **Great Longstone**.

Access by car: Turn off A6 on to A6020 near **Ashford**. Don't go into Ashford, but after 1 mile turn left under bridge on the lane to **Great Longstone**. Park unobstructively on street near **The Crispin Inn** or turn south and park on **Longstone Lane**.

> **Alternative start/finish**
> **Monsal Head** car park, walk along the lane through **Little Longstone**.

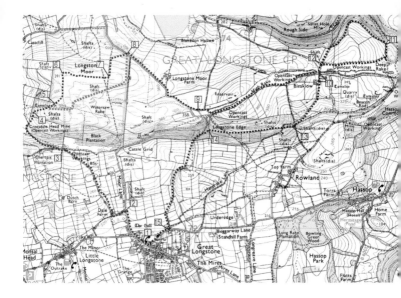

Our walk starts at **The Crispin Inn** (Wp.1), named after the patron saint of shoemakers, a traditional **Great Longstone** industry. We head north-west along the road towards **Little Longstone** until it turns west by an old pump where we continue ahead on **Moor Lane**, signed 'Longstone Edge'. Soon after we take the lane on the left (Wp.2 6M) signed 'Dale Farm'.

Past the farm buildings, the lane becomes a track which we follow round to the right to ascend (NW) along the walled track towards the high ground of **Longstone Edge**. The track levels off by a seat and shortly after we fork right through two gates (Wp.3 25M), with a signpost for a picnic area, and follow the track upwards past a new dewpond.

The new dewpond

Throughout this long ascent we are rewarded with panoramic views, south-east towards **Bakewell** and south-west towards **Monsal Head** and **Fin Cop**. At a wall by a wooded area we cross a stile into a pasture, then follow the wall uphill. A few years ago this pasture was a deep opencast mine, now restored and with little evidence of its mining history. West across **Hay Dale**, however, we can see opencast mining continuing further along the same *rake* or vein.

After the wall turns away, we follow a barbed wire fence north to an opening with an access land sign (Wp.4 40M) where we turn right to head north-east along a clear grassy path onto **Longstone Moor**. From the tumulus at the hilltop (Wp.5 45M), views open up to the west. To the north and east the ground is heather-covered, unusual for limestone country, due to the layer of poorly draining acidic soil left after the ice ages by the retreating icecap. Our route leaves the footpath and heads east north-east, taking advantage of sheep tracks where possible towards a gentle rise in the heather, passing evidence of lead mining. (Alternatively, remain on the footpath and follow it east north-east across the moor, to arrive at the cattle grid at Wp.8).

At the gentle rise we reach another tumulus (Wp.6 50M) and find ourselves at the western end of a gentle ridge, the ground falling away to the north across hummocky ground formerly intensively mined for lead. Beyond, is a classic Peak District view, the pattern of stone wall-enclosed fields of **Wardlow** and the **Hucklows** giving way to the darker forms of higher ground; the top of the **Mam Tor** landslip and the plateau of **Kinder Scout** lie beyond, and we can make out the plague village of **Eyam** and **The Barrel Inn** at **Bretton**, perched on **Eyam Edge**. Our route continues along the ridge (E) on pathless ground through heather, tussock-hopping across waterlogged ground. We reach and cross a path signed 'Foolow', soon reaching another path shortly after following the ruin of a stone wall (Wp.7 60M); turning left, we follow this path north. We descend from the moor, then fork right to follow another old wall east to approach a lane. A short distance to the right, a new gate by a cattle grid takes us onto a lane (Wp.8 65M).

The lane, widened to cope with mining lorries, takes us across open pastureland (SE) through the dip of **Watersaw Rake**, to reach the top of **Longstone Edge** after passing an opencast mine on the right. We take the very broad white track, (widened for use as a haul road for the mines) leaving the lane on the left (Wp.9 85M) to head east up the hill opposite.

(N.B. Several paths meet here, and to shorten the walk you could follow one of the paths heading south down the edge towards **Great Longstone**).

Bow Rake opencast workings

This track runs alongside the **High Rake** vein, formerly a rich source of lead, now being worked for Fluorspar, so for the next mile or so we're in close proximity to mine workings on our left: to the right, however, the views open up south-east towards **Chatsworth House** and the **Derwent Edges**. As we descend towards the farm at **Bleaklow**, the scale of the opencast workings at **Bow Rake** become apparent. A gash several hundred feet deep has been driven deep into the vein.

At **Bleaklow** a several paths and tracks converge (Wp.10 105M). We turn left through a gate, past a patch of cowslip-rich restoration fill, and cross over a stile to follow the footpath north-east between a barn and a dewpond and along a dip, then through a stile. The path starts descending into **Sallet Hole Dale** but we head right, following the wall and through a gate in a new fence, then along the top of a rock outcrop marking the rim of the dale, coming back to the wall and following it as it curves south-east, taking in views to **Eyam** and the gritstone edges above **Calver**. We stay with the wall, deviating only to avoid elder trees and nettles, until we pass through a stone stile at the head of the side dale (Wp.11 120M). We follow the wall south, then west through pastureland, with the recently completed **Deep Rake Mine** on our left, under restoration at the time of writing.

The path climbs over the shoulder of a hill before dropping down to the barn we passed earlier (Wp.12 140M) then turning left to return to the meeting of paths at **Bleaklow** (Wp.10). Continuing ahead, we pass to the left of the farm buildings. After heading south through a gate and into a field we descend to a stile, then head slightly to the right, crossing a shoulder of the hill to descend south-west across a scrub-encroached area. We come to a junction of tracks, and need to cast about for a bit to find our path opposite the junction, heading downhill through high gorse and then through a dip, to reach a walled track at a stile, where we go left. Ignoring the first stile on the right, we pass through a new gate on the right (Wp.13 165M), following a path alongside some old surface flurospar workings and noting the abandoned hand *trommel* screen.

Another gate takes us onto the open hillside. Ignoring the footpath descending to the left we ascend west to arrive at a track running alongside more recently restored mineworkings.

The track alongside Longstone Edge

The track (not shown on the Explorer map) forms a level terrace alongside **Longstone Edge** escarpment, with attractive views across the **Longstones** pastureland. Ignoring footpath signs on both sides, we follow it to and through a gate in a dip (Wp.14 180M), then taking a path to the left of the track.

... a stile onto pastureland ...

Shortly, we meet another path to descend off the edge and across a stile onto pastureland. We head for a rock outcrop with trees opposite, passing through a wicket gate and bearing right to pass along the bottom of the attractive little **Standhill Dale**. After passing through a few more gates our path arrives at **Beggarway Lane** on the edge of **Great Longstone** (Wp.15 195M). Turning right, we come to the church at a bend and take the path through the churchyard, bringing us out opposite the primary school. **The Crispin Inn**, the end of our walk, is a few steps to the right (Wp.1 200M). Refreshments can be had here or at **The White Lion** at the eastern end of the village.

24 HADDON & CHATSWORTH: Two Great Estates

The **Rivers Wye** and **Derwent** meet at **Rowsley**, their broad valleys providing a gentler and more pastoral landscape than the limestone plateau to the west or the gritstone moors to the east. The two great aristocratic houses and estates of **Haddon Hall** in the **Wye Valley**, and **Chatsworth House** on the banks of the **Derwent** are close by, though their proximity belies a great contrast.

Haddon Hall, owned by the Duke of Rutland, has for several centuries been subsidiary to the main seat at **Belvoir Castle**. Used only occasionally as a grand holiday home, it escaped the architectural fads and fashions of the aristocracy, so retains the ambience of a medieval hall locked in a time warp. Despite its commanding position on a bluff overlooking the **Wye**, it's a shy, retiring place. Public access to the estate is restricted to rights of way, though paying visitors can visit the house and garden. The rights of way are quiet; you're as likely to meet estate water bailiffs and gamekeepers going about their business as other visitors.

Chatsworth, by contrast, is exuberantly grand, splendidly located on the east bank of the **Derwent** in Capability Brown's landscaped park, overlooked by an 16th century hunting tower on a bluff above. A lot of England's history (and a wee bit of Scotland's as well) has been enacted in these grounds. Paying visitors can experience the lush, opulent aura of the house (enhanced by rather soft-porn ceiling frescoes) and its enclosed gardens and arboretum, with their fountains and cascades. Walkers have open access to most of the deer park, and concession paths give access to the woods and moors above the house.

The walk starts and finishes in **Rowsley** (though the **Calton Lees** car park would be as good for motorists) and heads over the rolling country behind **Haddon Hall** and along the **Wye Valley** into the outskirts of **Bakewell**. After traversing the high ground of **Calton Pastures** we descend through **Chatsworth Park** via the estate village of **Edensor** to the bridge over the **River Derwent** at **Chatsworth**, then follow the river valley through the deer park back to **Rowsley**. The walk could be combined with a visit to **Haddon Hall** or **Chatsworth House** - though muddy boots might be unwelcome.

3   4½H   10.6 miles/17km   330m / 330m   2

Safety Avice: 1. Deer can be dangerous if approached during the Autumn rutting season. 2. Bridleways are popular with mountain bikers.

Access by bus: R61 or TransPeak (**Bakewell-Matlock**, frequent) to Rowsley; or N°172 **Bakewell-Matlock** (Mon-Sat inc. B/H Mon, 2 hourly) to **Birchover**.

Alternative start/finish Calton Lees car park, by the B6012; **Bakewell**, the old station car park, via **Monsal Trail**.

Access by car: A6 to **Rowsley**: park at **Caudwell's Mill** or the shopping outlet car park and walk to **The Peacock Hotel** beside the A6 in the village. N.B. There may be restrictions and limited opening hours in either car park.

We start in front of **The Peacock Hotel** on the north side of the A6 in **Rowsley** (Wp.1). Taking the 'no through' road north-west next to the hotel, we pass the small post office and a farm track on the right (Wp.2 2M) where our return route will come in. A few yards after the end of the speed limit the road becomes a track (watch out for speeding tractors?) climbing out of the valley, providing views across to **Stanton Moor**, before running alongside **Bouns Corner Wood** to a metal vehicle barrier (Wp.3 18M). We take the left hand of the three tracks that diverge here through the wood, carpeted with bluebells in spring. Ignoring forest tracks on the right, we emerge into open country and descend slightly to another metal barrier (Wp.4 28M) and a junction.

The bridleway on the right is a short cut to the **Russian Cottage** (Wp.11) via **Calton Houses**, while the middle track leads directly down to **Coombs Viaduct** (Wp.8); we go left, our track running along a ridge with views of **Bakewell** down the valley on the right. At another track junction we go right for **Bakewell**. (N.B. If doing the walk in reverse, note that the other track, signed 'Rowsley' is <u>not</u> the one to follow, unless you want to walk alongside the A6.)

Our track runs alongside **Shadyside Plantation** on the right before curving south-west to follow a shelter belt. Where the main track bends left into a farm, we continue ahead on the marked bridleway, passing the old **Haddon Estate** bowling green and pavilion on the left. The bridleway bends west at a gate and follows the iron railing of **Haddon Park**, going through two more gates before dropping down to a gate onto a track. We turn left to follow the track downhill and round a sweeping hairpin corner. Through the fence on the right the blocked portal of the old **Haddon** railway tunnel can be seen, built to hide the **Derby-Manchester** railway beneath **Haddon Park**; sadly, its shallow depth in poor ground resulted in five deaths from cave-ins during its construction.

The bridge at Wp.6

The track descends to a bridge across the **River Wye** where a bridleway leaves on the right towards **Bakewell** (Wp.5 55M); we take the footpath just past it through a metal squeeze stile on the left, signed 'Haddon Hall'. Our path runs alongside the river with the **Haddon Park** railings on the left, giving good views across the park towards **Haddon Hall** in the distance, before passing through a willow wood and reaching a concrete bridge over the **River Wye** (Wp.6 60M), from where we retrace our steps to Wp.5. (If you want to visit **Haddon Hall**, the entrance is reached by continuing along this path and turning left at the A6).

From Wp.5 we take the bridleway opposite towards **Bakewell** along a grassy bank with a few old trees, passing duck decoy ponds in the wetlands by the river on the left, and the keeper's cottage on the right. Remaining on the bridleway (blue arrows), we ignore footpaths on the left. Instead, we head away from the river towards a gate in the opposite corner of the field below a wood (Wp.7 78M), then follow the track signed 'Bakewell', heading north round the toe of a ridge to reach **Coombs Road** as it passes under the viaduct (Wp.8 86M).

Crossing the lane, we climb steps up onto the old railway trackbed, signed 'Monsal Trail' to follow the trackbed as it sweeps round the hillside with views to **Bakewell**.

The building that resembles a giant eggbox is, appropriately, the new **Agricultural Business Centre**. After around a kilometre we pass under a bridge and climb steps up the bank on the right to reach a path (Wp.9 100M). The path across the bridge leads to **Bakewell**, amply provided with refreshments including the famous Bakewell Pudding. However our route follows the path east, uphill towards the wooded hillside ahead.

This area is frequented by swingers - of the golfing variety, of course - and our path runs straight across **Bakewell Golf Course**. Due care is needed: if a golfer is lining up a drive straight at us, we are probably safe, but if aiming to the left or the right of us, best beware! Having crossed the fairway, note the metal bell (see the photo on the nest page) to be used if going downhill to warn unsighted golfers of walkers approaching.

Once across the golf course, we enter **Manners Wood** (so no swearing please) and climb with the path through the attractive woodland, passing the concessionary woodland walk on the right, the steep wooded slope or *scarp* formed by gritstone. At the top we pass through a gate and into the meadows of **Calton Pastures**. Our path continues due east to the right of a small copse, then reaches a stile and gate to the right of a pond (Wp.10 120M). Just past the pond, we cross another stile and head gently downhill, parallel with a fence, aiming to the left of a copse in the valley floor, to pass through a gate in a fence and on to a grassy track.

The metal bell, Bakewell Golf Course

Edensor Church

The grassy track brings us to a junction with the bridleway from **Calton Houses** (Wp.11 135M); ahead in the corner of the field is **Russian Cottage** with its distinctive double gabled roof, built by a former duke for a visit by the Czar of Russia's family. Turning left along the bridleway, we pass through a belt of woodland to cross an improbably high stile and enter **Chatsworth Deer Park**. Our path continues straight ahead, running between plantations to descend towards the gritstone spire of **Edensor Church**.

We're free to roam on this section, and a detour to the left by **Maud's Plantation**, opens up views over the **Derwent Valley** and our first views of **Chatsworth House** with the Emperor Fountain to the right and the hunting tower on the bluff above.

Descending to **Edensor**, the path passes through a stile and on to a lane where we turn right to the centre of the village. Built to replace an older village nearer to the **Derwent** that spoiled the view from **Chatsworth House**, it is every bit an estate village, even down to the identical 'Chatsworth Blue' painted woodwork. The buildings have particularly fine stonework details - look out for the snake, the emblem of the Dukes of Devonshire, above the entrance to the old stables on the left. Refreshments can be found at the post office and tea room, to the east of the church.

Leaving the village by the cattle-grid gateway, (Wp.12 170M) we cross the busy B6012, but instead of taking the well-used path opposite we head north-east, straight up the slope opposite. This brings us to a new plantation, each tree with a commemorative plaque, and more views of **Chatsworth House**.

... a particularly good view of Chatsworth ...

We descend from the ridge by heading towards the hunting tower, which brings us to a bluff overlooking a bend in the **River Derwent** - a good picnic spot - with a particularly fine view of the bridge and the house behind before descending along the bluff to the bridge (Wp.13 190M).

Our onward route stays on this side of the **Derwent**, but a short detour across the bridge would bring us to the entrance to **Chatsworth House** and gardens.

The walled and moated structure to the left is **Queen Mary's Bower**, reputed (though the story may be embellished somewhat) to be the place where Mary Queen of Scots, kept as a political prisoner by the rather scary Bess of Hardwick (wife of the first Duke), was allowed to take the air under guard.

Queen Mary's Bower

From the bridge we follow the riverside path south across flat ground, then climb up over a small bluff to a terrace, past the weir. On approaching the ruined mill the path turns away from the river to reach the B6012 at the cattle grid (Wp.14 210M) and we take the lane south past **Calton Lees** car park and the garden centre. The lane curves right to reach a junction in **Calton Lees** village (Wp.15 230M). Ignoring the bridleway to **Calton Houses** we follow the lane due south to its end, then take the waymarked footpath across a stile to the left.

The footpath shortly drops down to the valley bottom and heads across several meadows, then passes through a muddy section of woodland, and joins a farm track, possibly muddy in sections, running alongside the **River Derwent**. Passing under an old railway bridge, beside the **Rowsley Viaduct**, the track joins the lane in **Rowsley** beside a farm (Wp.2). Turning left, we reach **The Peacock Hotel** at **Rowsley** in a few moments (Wp.1 270M) and have a range of options for refreshment in the village, including **The Peacock** and **Grouse and Claret** inns, **Caudwell's Mill** and the shopping centre.

25 CHATSWORTH:
The People's Aristocracy

A visitor may feel that the great house and estate of **Chatsworth** possess a timeless quality, unaffected by the centuries of technological and social change that have rolled past its grounds, like the waters of the **Derwent**. But to survive, this place has had to move with the times. By the latter half of the 20th century, the increasing cost of keeping the buildings and grounds in good order could no longer be borne by the private resources of the Cavendish family (hereditary holders of the title of Duke of Devonshire) so the ownership of the house and estate were transferred into a network of non-profit making charitable trusts. The Chatsworth House Trust is now responsible for funding the upkeep of the house and the home estate. The Duke of Devonshire pays a market rent for his family living quarters in the house, but the greater part of the huge cost of keeping the place in good order comes from the visitor's tourist dollar; there's no government subsidy.

Chatsworth has therefore become a kind of 'People's Aristocracy', reliant on income from its visitors, and it genuinely seems to welcome all, whether paying to visit the house and gardens or making free use of the deer park and surrounding countryside. A surprising amount of the home estate is freely accessible to walkers; all of Capability Brown's deer park both west of the **Derwent** and north of the house is open to the public to roam freely, and a network of concession paths allows visitors to walk through the woods and moors above the house - all this may surprise those brought up on the history of the Great Trespass.

There's enough to see and do at **Chatsworth** to fill the whole of a long weekend, including some serious walking. The route described here takes us onto moors and gritstone escarpments overlooking the house and the deer park to the east. As well as moorland walking, we pass through the deer park and ancient woodland, and are rewarded with views over the **Derwent** and **Wye Valleys** - all either on concession paths or open access. Please note that dogs must be kept on leads, that access is allowed only during the day, and that events such as the annual Chatsworth Show may require short term restrictions. Virtually none of the **Chatsworth** concession paths are marked on OS mapping, so to help those wanting to deviate from the walk described and do their own thing, I have mapped the network of concession paths and the open access area of the deer park as shown on the map extract.

Well worth a visit on the way home after the walk is the **Chatsworth Farm Shop**, in the old stud farm at **Pilsley**. Cheap it's not, and though some customers seem to come for the reflected aristocratic glory rather than the food, the range and quality of British food stocked is excellent.

1 · 4H · 8¾ miles/14km · 260m / 260m · 2

Safety Advice: Deer can be dangerous if approached during the autumn rutting season.

Access by bus: Several services through **Baslow** including N°170 **Bakewell-Chesterfield** (Hourly, 7 days/week), N°66 **Buxton- Chesterfield**, and N°X18 **Sheffield-Bakewell**, both 2 hourly 7 days/week.

Access by car: A619, A623, A621 to **Baslow** Park at **Baslow Car Park** (pay and display) at **Nether End**.
Alternative start/finish: **Robin Hood** car park, by **Robin Hood Inn** off A619 between **Baslow** and **Chesterfield**.

From the car park entrance at **Nether End** in **Baslow** (Wp.1), we turn right by the shop and head east across the old bridge.

The thatched cottage in Baslow

Across the bridge, we turn sharp right by a thatched cottage - a **Baslow** peculiarity, not found elsewhere in the Peak District - and follow the track through a gate until coming to the unusual rotating stile into the deer park, designed to let disabled visitors, but not able bodied deer, through.

Once in the deer park, several paths are signposted (Wp.2 4M). We take the left hand direction signed 'Robin Hood' and head east north-east across the parkland, crossing the tarmac drive. Reaching a fence by a track, we cross a stile beside a double gateway. A faint track runs due east from here, but we head slightly uphill and right of this track, towards some old oak trees to **Jubilee Rock**, a gritstone boulder with a dedication for Queen Victoria's golden jubilee (1887) carved into its face (Wp.3 15M); a herd of roe deer frequents this corner of the deer park. Following the contour of the hill east, we regain the grassy track and cross the deer park wall on a stile by a high gate (Wp.4 20M).

The path continues east through a pasture before crossing another stile and becoming a straight track through a wooded area, with power lines running alongside. Soon the track is running alongside the foot of a gritstone escarpment with the **Heathy Lea Brook** in a gorge on the left, before curving to the right and coming to a signpost at a junction of concession paths (Wp.5 30M). We ignore turnings left (from **Robin Hood Inn**, an alternative start point) and right, and continue ahead for a few yards until a post with a white arrow directs us to the right, away from the track. Several similar posts direct us across rough ground to a stile (Wp.6 35M) onto access land.

The concession path continues ahead, but we deviate from it, turning right and following a wall for a short distance before picking up a sheep track through the bracken, heading south towards a lone tree below a gritstone ridge, Past the tree, we climb up to a low dike running along the side of the ridge: ascending this, we find ourselves beside the artificial **Emperor Stream** created by Joseph Paxton to bring water into the park to power **The Cascade** and **The Emperor Fountain** beside **Chatsworth House**.

We turn left to walk alongside the stream, its elevated position providing views over the valley on the left. We pass an overflow sluice and around 200 metres later come to a track and turn right on it, crossing the stream on a small bridge (Wp.7 45M).

The track ascends steadily onto **Gibbet Moor**, at first south-west across open country and later running alongside a wall on our right. Ignoring gates on the right through the wall as it turns south beside some barns, we keep on this track for around 3 km as it ascends to the top of a ridge, where the wall on our right turns to descend from the ridge by a signpost (Wp.8 90M). Here, we deviate a short distance to the left to a fenced enclosure containing the rather under-whelming remains of a tumulus, **Hob Hurst's House** (Wp.9 93M). To the south-east is the gritstone **Harland Edge** and the high ground of **Beeley Moor**, designated access land, but this would add little to our enjoyment so we return to the signpost at Wp.8 and take the concession path following the wall south-west off the ridge. After crossing a ladder stile we come to a railway sleeper bridge over a stream (Wp.10 100M) where there's a three way fork of paths.

The track at Wp.11

We take the middle fork and continue south-west across the moor, passing a stone circle on the right before joining a broader track (Wp.11 115M), where we turn left to descend to a stile by a gate (Wp.12 120M) where we have a choice of two alternatives to our main route.

Alternative Route A
Follow the footpath into the woods opposite, then fork right on a rough path that descends alongside the **Beeley Brook** into **Beeley**. Refreshments may be had at **The Devonshire Arms**, returning to **Baslow** on the footpath from the B6012 opposite **Beeley Church**, crossing fields to **One Arch Bridge** near **Calton Lees**. Crossing it, and taking the footpath alongside the **River Derwent** through the deer park via **Chatsworth Bridge**.

Alternative Route B
Turn right on the track, which leads directly to **One Arch Bridge** via **Beeley Hilltop Farm**, then follow Alternative A.

Our route returns along the track towards Wp.11, though we deviate slightly to the left to walk along the rim of the edge, taking in views across the **Derwent** and **Wye Valleys** towards **Stanton Moor**. We follow the edge north-west, parallel to the track, as it descends gently towards the woodland ahead. This moor, named **Rabbit Warren**, is where rabbits were farmed after being introduced to **Chatsworth** in the middle ages. We rejoin the track where the path from **Beeley Hilltop** farm comes in from the left (Wp.13 145M), passing shortly afterwards through a gate and into the woods.

The track curves to the right by an ancient Beech tree and comes to a crossroads (Wp.14 148M) where we will turn left. The alternative, continuing ahead, would take us past **Swiss Lake** and **Emperor Lake** to rejoin the route near the hunting tower (Wp.19). Having turned left, we follow a tarmac lane north-west until the road bends sharp left at a hairpin corner (Wp.15 155M); we follow the path opposite leading north into the woods, running alongside the gritstone edge and revealing, through Oak, Beech and Silver Birch trees, occasional glimpses of **Chatworth House** below.

This path emerges by a waterfall (Wp.16 166M), another of Joseph Paxton's creations, this is the water that feeds **The Cascade** in the park below, visible through the trees. Ascending steps on the right, we reach a track, turn left then right again, bringing us to the south end of **Emperor Lake**, constructed as the header reservoir for the water features in the park below, and frequented by waterfowl (Wp.17 170M).

The Elizabethan Hunting Tower

Returning to the track, we turn right and head north, then take a faint path on the left by a very old Beech, bringing us back onto the path along the gritstone edge rim, then emerging at the foot of the Elizabethan **Hunting Tower** (Wp.18 175M), built to provide panoramic views of the deer park so that the matriarch of the Cavendish family, Bess of Hardwick, could watch the deer hunting. It's now a holiday let.

Leaving the tower (N), we pass a maintenance yard and meet the tarmac lane coming in from the right from **Swiss Lake** (Wp.19 178M).

Continuing north along it, we pass a footpath on the left (Wp.20 185M, a direct route back to **Beeley**) before reaching a crossroads (Wp.21 195M). The tarmac forks left while we continue straight ahead on a track, then bearing left to follow the concession path over a high stile in the deer park wall. The path runs alongside the wall, but we bear left to follow the rim of the gritstone **Dobb Edge** enjoying views across the **Derwent Valley** towards **Baslow** and beyond until a green track descends from the rim to run alongside the crags. Abandoned millstones and other carved items can be seen amongst the gritstone boulders, relics of gritstone quarrying.

The abandoned gritstone quarry

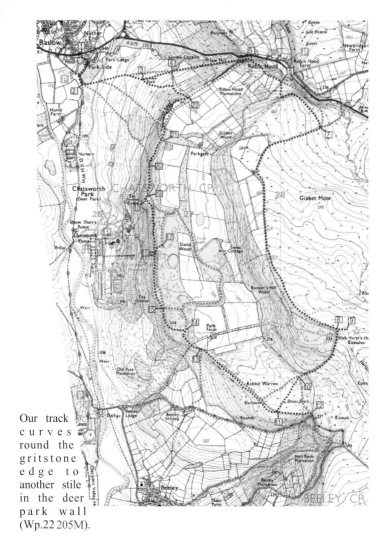

Our track curves round the gritstone edge to another stile in the deer park wall (Wp.22 205M).

The path over the stile leads to **Robin Hood Inn**, while we turn left before the stile to follow an old hollow track down the hill, then bear left to head in a beeline towards **Baslow** in the valley below, bringing us back to **Jubilee Rock** (Wp.3 220M) from where we retrace our steps into **Baslow** (Wp.1 240M). Several establishments offer refreshments, including **Sweet Jean's** shop and **The Café on the Green** by the car park, and **The Devonshire** and **Cavendish Hotels**. No idea how they got those names!

26 THE DRAGON'S BACK: 19th September 2004

This new walk deserves to become a Peak District classic. Its relatively modest 13 km/4 hour length belies a series of strenuous ascents and careful descents, punctuated with broad vistas across the upper Dove valley. Our route traverses the length of the distinctive **Chrome** and **Parkhouse** (Dragon's Back) **Hills**, whose jagged outline punctuates the scenery between **Buxton** and **Longnor**. Their distinctive sharp edged landform was created 325 million years ago as coral reefs in the Carboniferous sea.

19 September 2004 is significant as the day that 'Right to Roam'(Countryside and Rights of Way Act) came into force. This allowed, for the first time, access to the distinctive **Dragon's Back**, which previously had been disfigured by 'Keep Out' signs. A significant and appropriate date for me too, as this walk started my field research for this book.

Longnor is not well known but it's an excellent place to end a walk, with four pubs and several cafés to choose from, and it is worth a few minutes pottering around the narrow streets and alleys of this former market town in which time seems to have stood still for a couple of centuries. This underrated corner of the Peak District deserves to be better known.

Safety Advice: Do not attempt in hill fog. **Parkhouse Hill** is extremely steep sided, slippery, and has poorly defined paths. Do not attempt this section if a vertigo sufferer, inexperienced in mountain walking, or if not wearing adequate footwear.

Access by bus: 442 **Buxton-Ashbourne** service (2 hourly, 7 days) to **Longnor**.

> **Alternative start/finish**
> **Hollinsclough** or **Earl Sterndale**

Access by car: B5053 to **Longnor**. Park in the square or (unobstructively) on street in the village. Parking in square fills up quickly at weekends.

We start in **Longnor Square** (Wp.1 0M) by taking the narrow street that runs uphill (NNE) from the chip shop café. Crossing another road, we take the lane diagonally across to the left, and then the signed footpath to head (N) over a stile and across a field (NE) to another stile at the crest of the ridge (5M). Below us a concrete track curves round to the right, but our path takes a zigzag course down the ridge to join the track by an old drystone platform, where we turn left (Wp.2 10M) (in reverse, look out for this as there is no waymark).

At the bottom of the hill our track passes a stone barn on the left. We leave the track to go left and then right through gates to round the barn. Now we follow a bridleway (NE) across the meadows, towards a distinctive gap in the hills opposite; very muddy in wet weather. Passing over a low ridge, we cross the **River Dove** on the **Beggar's Bridge** to continue towards the gap. This is **Green Lane**, a wide drovers' route between hedges with the distinctive forms of **Parkhouse** and **Chrome Hills** on our left.

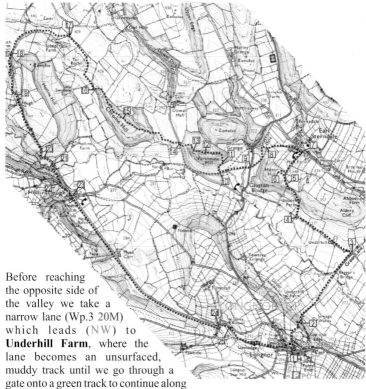

Before reaching the opposite side of the valley we take a narrow lane (Wp.3 20M) which leads (NW) to **Underhill Farm**, where the lane becomes an unsurfaced, muddy track until we go through a gate onto a green track to continue along the foot of the hills, taking a footpath opposite a house (Wp.4 30M) to climb (N) steeply up the ridge to a wall which we follow (NW) to a stile (Wp.5 40M). Crossing the stile, we continue alongside a wall on our right for two minutes, then head off left, aiming for the highest ground, the top of **Hitter Hill** (Wp.6 45M), offering panoramic views over **Parkhouse** and **Chrome Hills** and the upper **Dove Valley**.

We leave the hill top (NW), passing old lead working hollows in the hilltop and shortly a stile comes into view which we cross into a field holding a range of animals including donkeys and Jacob's Sheep, to follow the path (NNE) towards a smallholding. Following the path towards **Earl Sterndale**'s church tower, dodging chickens and cockerels, the 'smallholding' turns out to be the **Quiet Woman Pub**; a rather good pint, if it's open.

Just before our path reaches the road in front of the pub (Wp.7 52M) we take the **Hollinsclough** path off to the left (W) to pass through three gates, gently climbing out of **Earl Sterndale** with the tops of **Chrome** and **Parkhouse Hills** ahead. Our path curves (WSW) as it brings us up to a stile at the top of **Glutton Dale** (Wp.8 60 M), where it's worth taking a few moments to admire the view and locate the route ahead.

Across the awkward stile we have two choices: straight ahead (SSW), making directly for the stile near the foot of the hill, or right (W) on an ancient packhorse track which shortly zigzags (S) to reach the same stile; more interesting and easier. At the foot of the hill, we follow the path through the stile and across the field to a pair of stiles (Wp.9 68M) which we go carefully through, leading us across the B5053.

Following the waymarked path across the fields (W) through a stile, we head to the south of **Parkhouse Hill** which now towers above us, resisting the temptation to short cut to the foot of the ridge. Instead we keep on until we cross a stile with the 'Marooned Hiker' waymark indicating that we are on Right to Roam land (Wp.10 70M). This is where the ascent of **Parkhouse Hill**, the **Dragons Back**, begins (if you decide not to ascend it, go straight on (W) on the path around the foot of the hill, then joining an unfenced lane and following it until you meet the cattle grid at Wp.14). We turn right (N), following the wall until it turns east, then 150 yards later (Wp.11), before the wall starts to descend, we head very steeply due north up the side of the hill, until we reach the ridge. We head along, or just to the left (S) of, the crest of the ridge (W) to reach the summit (Wp.12 80M) and pause to look at the view, including the path we will later follow up **Chrome Hill**, to the west.

To descend we continue (W) along the ridge, but halfway down (Wp.13 88M) the ridge becomes impossible to traverse directly. Going right (N), we descend carefully by means of a rocky terrace and then sheep tracks which zigzag (NW) down to a grassy hollow, then along the foot of the hill (W). Finally we reach a small lane near a cattle grid (Wp.14 95M). Teas may be available at weekends in **Dowall Hall**, if we detour 300 yards north along this lane.

Just before the cattle grid a stile takes us onto the 'High Edge via Chrome Hill' path (not shown on the OS Explorer map) which takes us uphill initially, to the south of the main ridge, and to a stile by a tree where we re-enter 'right to roam' land.

Parkhouse Hill, from between Wps. 14&15

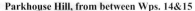

Through the stile, we follow the path (WNW) straight up the ridge of **Chrome Hill**; it's worth pausing just after the stile to admire the view of **Parkhouse Hill**.

After a 'puff and grunt' ascent, we reach the summit of **Chrome Hill** (443 m Wp.15 125M), the highest point of our route.

We leave the summit of **Chrome Hill** and head north-west, descending to the first wind gap, then we follow the path to the right of the ridge, switching to the left hand side of the ridge by a small cave or natural arch. Ultimately our path passes to the right of the ridge and follows a stone wall down off the hill. This turns to the south-west for a short descent before a stile is reached, with the concessionary path waymarked to cross it (Wp.16 135M).

Following the waymarked path (NW) alongside a wall we cross two stiles before it turns (N) to climb steeply to the top of the plateau, where it turns (NW) again and crosses more stiles before the concessionary path ends at a signposted junction of paths by a cattle grid (Wp.17 150M).

We take the 'Booth Farm' path (W) to cross a number of stiles and gates before joining a farm track, becoming tarmacked as we stroll along to a junction of tracks (Wp.18 160M) at the edge of **Booth Farm**. Leaving the tarmac, we take the waymarked bridleway on the left to head carefully over a cattle grid (S); note the change of geology as we pass from limestone to the Millstone Grit Series.

We follow this bridleway along a track (S) until we reach **Fough Cottage** where a choice of paths presents itself (Wp.19 166M). We could take either, but the main bridleway, which passes on the uphill side of the cottage (slightly E of S) is the best option. Tracks fork off the bridal path to the left (E); our route keeps going downhill, so any uphill track is a wrong turn. Where the track ahead is labelled 'no access' (Wp.20, our path heads off the track to the right, following a stone wall through bracken. The waymarkers are confusing here: we ignore the bridleway (blue arrow, SW) and continue (SE) for 30 yards until we reach a stone wall.

Here we turn right (S) to be confronted with one of the strangest field gates in the **Peak District**, made out of an old wrought iron garden gate mounted in a scaffolding frame with steps up to it made out of stonecrusher screen, all painted white. After the gate (Wp.21 180M) we descend to a packhorse bridge (the parapets were low so the horse's panniers could overhang them) and then ascend the slope opposite diagonally (SE) to come through a gate onto a lane (Wp.22 190M) where we turn left (SE) to stroll down to **Hollinsclough** village; unfortunately, no refreshment facilities.

The 'garden gate' at Wp.21

At the village centre (Wp.23) we continue straight ahead (SE) along a lane, past the phone box, ignoring the left turn past the school.

This straight lane with wide verges is little used, making for an easy stroll to a T-junction (Wp.24 220M) where we turn left. Just round the corner is a footpath sign by an awkward stile (Wp.25 223M). Over the stile, we head (ESE) across the fields, passing through a number of squeeze stiles before joining a rough tarmac track at **Gauledge Farm** (in reverse, look for the waymark: if you reach the farmyard gate, you've missed it). Heading along the track brings us back across the B5053 to **Longnor**'s square (Wp.1 240M) and a welcome pint or cup of tea in one of the many pubs or cafés available.

27 BUXTON TO LONGNOR:
The Lost Peak District of the Buxton Salient

Though the small agricultural town of **Bakewell** is often called the capital of the Peak District, **Buxton** would have a far greater claim on this title, were it not for its deliberate exclusion from the National Park. **Buxton** has flourished since Roman times, first as a mineral water spa, then as an inland resort and a centre for local industry such as lime making and quarrying. It has always been the centre of communications and commerce for the High Peak, and its fine Georgian and Victorian buildings, many paid for by profits from the copper and lead mining of the Peak District, befit the role.

The 20th century was rather unkind to the town, as mineral water spas became unfashionable and the grand crescents, pavilions and gardens became run down and under-used. Perhaps the cruellest cut came in 1951 when the National Park boundaries were drawn, excluding not only the scarred quarrying areas and wartime military land, but also the town itself. This misguided decision, taken to keep the Park's population - and its influence on decision making - at a minimum, left **Buxton** in its **Salient**, surrounded by yet separated from its Peak District hinterland.

But regeneration efforts have meant a brighter start to the 21st century, with The Pavilion and its ornamental gardens restored, and new uses found for the Georgian and Victorian buildings. Its separation from the rest of the Peak District by the artifice of boundaries and by quarries and wartime military land, remains, but with the military gone and the quarries becoming worked out, the new century brings an opportunity to reclaim this land. It is time to reconnect **Buxton** with the Peak District.

This walk allows us to make our own connection, by walking from the attractive urban environment of **Buxton** to the dramatic limestone reef country and rural ambience of **Longnor**. In between, we pass through **Grinlow Wood** and **Quarry**, examples of how derelict land can be successfully reclaimed, and through the edge of the former military zone. Originally part of a munitions storage facility, it was used to burn surplus mustard gas after the war, and the concrete burn pads are now used by the Health and Safety Executive for explosion and flame research. Imagine, between the bangs and whooshes, how with relatively modest effort this area could be reclaimed for the Peak District.

This walk is best done in the direction described (from town to country), passing along the crest of **Chrome Hill** before finishing in **Longnor**. The range of pubs and cafés there allows us to take refreshment whilst waiting for the N°442 bus for the return journey to **Buxton** - a scenic ride through the upper **Dove Valley** and the villages of **Crowdecote** and **Earl Sterndale**, before passing the quarries of **Hindlow** to return into **Buxton**.

Safety Advice: 1. The walk passes through the Health and Safety Laboratory Explosion and Flame Testing area. Quite safe - provided you keep to the marked paths, heed the warning notices and follow instructions.

Access by train: From **Manchester** and **Stockport** to **Buxton**.

Access by bus: Several services to **Buxton**. N°442 (**Ashbourne** to **Buxton**, 2 hourly, 7 days/week) to **Longnor**.

Access by car: Main roads to **Buxton**. Park in **Pavilion Gardens** car park (pay parking), along **Burlington Road** (Wp.3) or the free **Poole's Cavern** car park (Wp.4). A515/B5053 to **Longnor**, limited free parking in **Market Square**.

If arriving by train or bus, we cross the **Relief Road (Station Road)** outside **Buxton Station** at the Pelican crossing (Wp.1) and turn right, then left down **Station Approach**, now a cul-de-sac, opposite the **Palace Hotel**. At the bottom of the hill we cross the main road at the lights and continue on the road opposite, passing the grand Georgian buildings of **The Crescent** on our right.

On the left, just after an arts centre, is **St Anne's Well**, a continuous stream of free mineral water - slightly warm - gushing from the lion's head: a good place to fill your water bottle (Wp.2 4M). Past the well, we turn right by **Old Hall Hotel** and arrive in front of **The Opera House** (Wp.3 6M), turning left before it onto a pedestrian terrace between **The Buxton Pavilion** on the right and **The Pavilion Gardens** on the left, both recently restored.

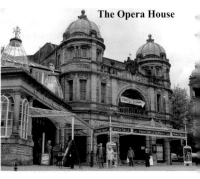

The Opera House

There's more than one way through the gardens to emerge at the southern apex where **Burlington Road** meets the **Broad Walk**; one way is to bear left before the car park at the end of the terrace, to descend to a footbridge. Bearing left again past a play area, we reach a large duck pond and go round it clockwise. (This was the scene of my own walk-on part in the town's regeneration, testing the silt in the pond for contaminants; not the highest point of my professional career, as we got our sampling technician stuck up to his waist in the silt - neat duck droppings - and nearly had to call the Fire Brigade out to rescue him!)

On the far side of the pond we head for the southern exit, neat Victorian villas facing **Broad Walk** on our left. We cross **Burlington Road**, then **Macclesfield Road** at the pelican crossing (Wp.4 20M). Taking **Temple Road**, the right of two roads ahead (ignoring the brown sign for 'Poole's Cavern'), we turn left after passing **Buxton College** (still **Temple Road**), to reach **Green Lane**. Crossing into **Poole's Cavern** car park and keeping to the right, we find the footpath leading into **Grin Low Wood** (Wp.5 30M).

After ascending steps we bear left on the footpath signed 'Solomon's Temple' and climb the stony path through natural deciduous woodland; not so natural, actually; two hundred years ago this was an industrial wasteland.

The 'natural' deciduous woodland

Over a million tons of lime waste was dumped on this hillside. The lime burners and their families actually lived in caves hollowed out in the waste, which must have made the place look like something out of The Lord of the Rings. In 1820 the Duke of Devonshire planted **Grin Low Wood** to reclaim the land and improve the environs of **Buxton**. As we ascend through the woods, the waste heaps can still be seen, now tree covered and returned to nature.

At the top of the wood we pass through a squeeze stile and head across hummocky ground (the result of lime burning) to the round tower at the top of the hill (Wp.6 45M SE) called either **Solomon's Temple** or **Grinlow Tower**. It's well worth ascending the tower's spiral staircase to enjoy panoramic views north over **Buxton** with **Comb's Moss** beyond, south to **Harpur Hill** and its industrial estate on former military land, east to limestone country, and the gritstone heights of **Axe Edge** to the west.

Leaving the tower, we retrace our steps to the stile but instead of crossing back into the wood we continue alongside the wall, passing through a gate and bearing left into a rock cutting to reach a footpath sign (Wp.7 50M). Ignoring the path right, we continue ahead (an old quarry void on our right), to head west on a grassy ridge towards **Axe Edge**. This artificial ridge was formed from waste tips by Derbyshire County Council in the 1970s and screens the quarry workings to our right, now a caravan site. Turning left at the access road, we follow it to the main entrance by old weighbridge buildings.

At the entrance (Wp.8 65M) we carefully cross the fast **Grin Low Road** and take the footpath opposite, heading along a farm track (S). The pastureland to our right changes from green, short grazed grass to longer, rougher brown grass and bracken marking the boundary between limestone and gritstone at the **Stanley Moor Fault**. As the farm track descends into the valley we pass a large earthen embankment, formerly the dam for the **Stanley Moor Reservoir**, now cut down and the reservoir drained. Its abandonment may be due to its Victorian builders inadvertently siting the dam on top of the fault line.

After crossing a bridge (Wp.9 75M) we leave the farm track to bear right onto a green path heading south around the shoulder of **Anthony Hill**. The path reaches a crest, then descends into a dip alongside the old **Cromford and High Peak Railway** track, now carrying a private road. On the far side of the dip we enter a wood at a kissing gate by a large 'Danger' sign - the explosion and flame research area, so listen out for bangs and whooshes!

The path takes us to the top of the wood where we reach the road, running along the old railway track (Wp.10 90M); we turn left. On the right, some of the burn pads and other paraphernalia can be seen. In a few yards, at a crossroads with extremely large footpath signs, we go straight on, though a brief detour up the road on the right to the old **Turncliff Farm** would allow inquisitive folks a closer look at the research area.

Shortly, before the old railway starts to cross a high embankment over a valley, we fork right at another large green footpath sign (Wp.11 95M) onto another old railway trackbed, now a green path taking us along a low cutting then over a short embankment, ignoring a footpath right. After a straight section it abruptly turns left past a 'No Admittance' sign (Wp.12 105M); just before it turns, we fork right and through a gate to head into a small valley (S), crossing a ladder stile and ascending, a fence to our right.

Just after the path crosses a ruined wall we go over a stile in the fence on our right and head diagonally across the field towards timber fencing by a lane, crossing another stile and turning left (Wp.13 115M). At the road junction after a cattle grid we fork left (Wp.14 120M), following the lane past **High Edge** stock car racing track and a series of disused munitions storage bunkers on the left, to cross a stile in the fence on the right (Wp.15 130M) onto access land.

The limestone pavement

We head directly uphill onto **High Edge**, aiming for its highest point at the top of the ridge marked by a pillbox. Following the crest of the edge (SE), we pass an area of limestone pavement - unusual in the Peak District - and head for another pillbox on the southern summit, but a fence blocks our way just before reaching it; we have to cross it close to the crags; those more cautious may

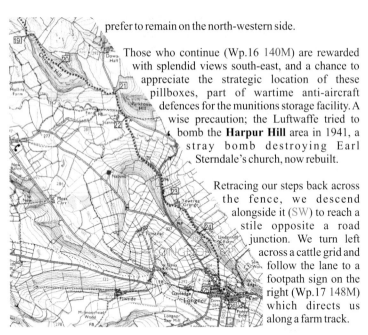

prefer to remain on the north-western side.

Those who continue (Wp.16 140M) are rewarded with splendid views south-east, and a chance to appreciate the strategic location of these pillboxes, part of wartime anti-aircraft defences for the munitions storage facility. A wise precaution; the Luftwaffe tried to bomb the **Harpur Hill** area in 1941, a stray bomb destroying Earl Sterndale's church, now rebuilt.

Retracing our steps back across the fence, we descend alongside it (SW) to reach a stile opposite a road junction. We turn left across a cattle grid and follow the lane to a footpath sign on the right (Wp.17 148M) which directs us along a farm track.

Across a cattle grid, we go left at a junction of paths (Wp.18 150M), the concession path signed 'Glutton Bridge via Chrome Hill' (the next section is, in reverse, part of Walk 26). This passes south-east across several stiles before turning to the right and descending a grassy slope. Note the hollow ground to the right, a *shack* or swallow hole, where the small stream disappears underground as it meets the limestone. Close to the bottom of the slope, the path goes through a stile on the left and runs alongside a wall before reaching a stile into access land (Wp.19 165M).

The path turns left and ascends alongside the wall (NE) before curving right and ascending (SE) along the ridge of **Chrome Hill**, running first to the left and later to the right of the ridge's sharp crest.

Shortly after passing a cave which pierces the ridge we attain the summit of **Chrome Hill** (Wp.20 180M). Our descent follows the ridge south-east, with views of **Parkhouse Hill**, all the way down to the lane by a cattle grid in **Dowel Dale** (Wp.21 195M) where we turn right.

... a cave which pierces the ridge ...

(An optional ascent of **Parkhouse Hill** can be made, heading to the left of the pinnacle to attain the ridge, descending at the far end of the ridge to return to Wp.22 along a public footpath).

The lane runs along the foot of **Parkhouse Hill** until a track comes in from the right, shortly after which we reach a stile in the fence on our right at the second of three footpath signs (Wp.22 200M). Across the stile, we head across the pasture (SSE), crossing the **River Dove** on a footbridge before ascending the far side to a stile between a farmhouse and an electricity pole, then following the farm track to reach the B5054.

The settlement in the valley on our left is **Glutton Bridge**, the large building once a creamery, built - literally - by a co-operative of dairy farmers in the 1930s to end their dependence on private milk buyers. After the war, the Milk Marketing Board took over milk distribution and the creamery was abandoned; now, it has come full circle with milk distribution privatised again, farm gate milk prices at an all time low, and farmers powerless in the market.

We bear right alongside the B5054 and ascend towards traffic lights past **High Acres** with its interesting arrangement of front and back doors on different storeys because of the slope, then turn left at a farm gate signed for 'Yewtree Grange' (Wp.23 215M). The path bears right before the farm and follows the electricity poles south-east to a cattle grid with a stile on the right which we cross to run alongside a fence, with the driveway to a house on the far side. Past the house, the path crosses a stile on the right and ascends (SE) towards a farmhouse, joins a track, then meets a junction of tracks by the farmhouse entrance (Wp.24 225M).

We turn left following a footpath sign, and descend along a track to a gate with a squeeze stile on the right. Through the squeeze stile, our path ascends the slope (SW) to meet a stile at the top with views across the **Dove Valley**. Crossing the stile, the path heads south across a field to a stile by houses, then drops to a narrow lane where we bear left to emerge on **Church Street** in **Longnor** (Wp.25 235M).

Crossing diagonally left, we follow a cobbled alleyway down steps, past **The Red Bull Gallery**, to emerge in the market square at the end of our walk (Wp.26 240M). Whilst waiting for the bus to take us back into **Buxton** (the bus stop is opposite **The Crewe and Harpur Arms**) we have several options for refreshments in the town's pubs or cafés.

28 DANE BRIDGE, GRADBACH & LUDS CHURCH:
Icebergs & Wallabies, Heretics & Highlanders

What's the connection between **The Ship** pub at **Wincle**, as far from the sea as you can get, Australian marsupials living wild on the Staffordshire moors, and a once-prominent local family? Sounds like a dodgy pub quiz question, but it reveals a fascinating footnote of local history. The pub sign, a three masted ship surrounded by icebergs, gives a clue.

The answer is the Antarctic explorer, Sir Ernest Shackleton, who sailed his ship, HMS Nimrod, on the 1907-9 expedition to Antarctica, before his ill-fated Endurance expedition of 1914-6. Sir Philip Brocklehurst of nearby **Swythamley Hall** accompanied Shackleton on the Nimrod as assistant geologist, and returning via Australia, brought back wallabies for **Swythamley's** private zoo; the pub was dedicated to his adventure. At the onset of the second world war, with food short, the zoo animals were released onto the moors to fend for themselves. For a while the wallabies prospered and bred, startling many a walker.

The Brocklehursts were an adventurous lot. Sir Philip later became the first person to cross the Sahara Desert in a motor car while his brother, Henry Courtney Brocklehurst, after First World War service as one of the first members of the Royal Flying Corps, became game warden of the Sudan. Returning to military service in the Second World War, he was killed 'on commando' in Burma in 1942. His memorial plaque is on the prominent gritstone formation of **Hanging Stone**.

Sadly, the wallabies are no more, and the moors are left to their native fauna. The Brocklehursts, too, are gone from **Swythamley Hall**.

Nearby is the atmospheric **Luds Church**, a deep crevasse in the gritstone of **Back Forest**, the result of a huge gritstone mass sliding on softer shales beneath. This chasm, concealed from passing eyes, has long been a hiding place, and in the 15th century was used as a church by the Lollard sect, early nonconformists branded as heretics by the Catholic Church. Despite the name, it has no connection with the machine-breaking Luddites.

In 1745 this area was part of Scotland for a few days as Bonnie Prince Charlie's highlanders passed through on their way to Derby, and passed through again at the beginning of their retreat to Culloden. Fragments of this history remain: local signposts to Royal Cottage identify a house on the moors where the Young Pretender spent a night, and the Saltire flies over **Ashbourne** every July as Scots assemble for a highland gathering - presumably keen to reclaim the Peak District for Scotland.

This walk is deservedly a classic, for as well as the fascinating local history it opens up some excellent gritstone walking country. It takes us from **Dane Bridge**, past **Hanging Stone** and through **Luds Church**, on to the **Back Forest** ridge and to the north western end of **The Roaches**. We cross a valley to **Gradbach Hill** on a new route opened up by Right to Roam, before dropping back to the **River Dane** at **Gradbach Mill**, returning along the valley to **Dane Bridge**. Unfortunately, there's no bus access to this walk - the only walk in this book without any - though it could be combined with Walk 29 and its summer Sunday bus access to **The Roaches**.

Safety Advice: 1. Be alert for hidden crevasses around **Luds Church**. 2. Claustrophobia sufferers should avoid the path through **Luds Church**.

Alternative start
The Roaches (combined with Walk 29)

Access by car: Turn south off the A54 (**Congleton-Buxton**) by **The Crossroads Motel** at **Cleulow Cross**, follow the minor road to **Wincle** and **Dane Bridge**. Park unobstructively on street between **The Ship Inn** and **Dane Bridge** (limited space).

We start at the bridge over the **River Dane**, astride the Cheshire-Staffordshire border between the Cheshire village of **Wincle** and the Stafffordshire hamlet of **Dane Bridge** (Wp.1). Heading into Staffordshire (SW), we take the second footpath on the left, a narrow alley between walls, leading shortly onto a drive at the front of a house. A waymarked path (an alternative route to Wp.4) goes straight ahead while we turn right along the drive, then left at the entrance to another drive, followed by an immediate right to a stile (Wp.2 4M).

The lane through semi-parkland

Through the stile, we enter parkland and climb south on an old tree-lined track to a lane by the stone slab-roofed **Snipe House** (Wp.3 8M), where we turn left. The lane takes us through a pastoral, semi-parkland scene, with views left across the **Dane Valley** towards **Shutlingsloe**. After passing **Park House** it becomes a gravel track (ignore the track on the left), and a glimpse of **Swythamley Hall** can soon be had over a gate to the right.

Hanging Stone

Soon afterwards the track changes direction from east to north and we ascend gradually to a junction of tracks (Wp.4 28M), a ridge and the distinctive **Hanging Stone** ahead.

We cross a stile opposite, and follow the signposted concession path to **Hanging Stone**, a block of gritstone jutting out from the side of the ridge (Wp.5 35M). Similar blocks of gritstone, often strangely shaped and whimsically named, are found all over gritstone country, some quirk of geology over 280 million years making them more erosion resistant than the surrounding rock. Noting the two plaques mounted on the rock, one commemorating a Brocklehurst, the other a mastiff dog, we mount the path to the top of the stone and admire views across to **The Roaches**, **Gun Hill** and the scattered farms of **Leekfrith**.

The path continues across moorland (ENE), to a well-used path at a stile where we bear left, cross another stile and come to another junction of paths (Wp.6 40M); on the right is an airy ridge walk over **Back Forest** to Wp.10, but we take the path ahead signed 'Gradbach', following a wall contouring round the hillside, eventually coming to woodland and meeting a junction of paths by a rocky tor (Wp.7 50M); we take the right fork signed 'Luds Church'.

Luds Church

The entrance to **Luds Church**, reached in about five minutes, could easily be missed. It's on the right, just past a short wooden fence, and appears to disappear into the hillside (Wp.8 55M; if you're claustrophobic, continue ahead for a few yards and take a path on the right to bypass the crevasse). Taking the path into the rocks we follow the crevasse, descending into a large gap between two massive gritstone rock faces. It's a sobering thought that this unique natural feature was created by the movement of the huge masses of rock on both sides of us! The depths of this crevasse see little sun, and it has its own micro-ecosystem of mosses and ferns.

Ascending at the chasm's end, we follow the path through woodland (SE). Shortly after the path descends into a dip we divert south-west, leaving the forest (Wp.9 65M). Our faint path leads to a dip in the ridge (Wp.10 70M) where we bear left to follow the ridge path, reaching a lane at **Roach End** where several paths converge (Wp.11 90M). The path opposite continues up the ridge to **Roaches Top**, then along the ridge (described in Walk 29), and is an optional there-and-back addition to this walk. However, our onward route follows the bridleway, descending along the partly surfaced farm track (NNE).

Past the farm, the track becomes a worn path and drops into the valley, crossing **Black Brook** at a footbridge before ascending east alongside a wall, the gritstone edge of **Gradbach Hill** to the north. Where an old wall comes in from the left (Wp.12 110M) we turn left to follow the crest of the edge (N) to a new gate leading onto a track (Wp.13 120M).

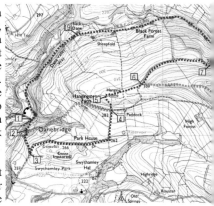

We turn left, then almost immediately bear right by a marker post on a faint path to continue following the edge of **Gradbach Hill**, heading for a distinctive rock jutting out from the edge (Wp.14 125M). This airy route along the edge's rim descends gradually from this rock. Keep an eye out for a small wooden post marking a concessionary path (Wp.15 133M), the start of our route off the hill (SW) following a line of posts to a wicket gate.

The distinctive rock

The route then runs alongside a wall to meet a farm track, a public footpath. We turn right and head north through a farmyard (also used as an architectural salvage store) to a stile by a gate at a junction of tracks (Wp.16 140M). (The track left is a short cut to Wp.18.) We follow the track ahead (which becomes a lane) around the shoulder of the hill, reaching a junction (Wp.17 145M) to turn sharp left onto the lane leading down to the Youth Hostel at **Gradbach Mill**, a tranquil spot beside the **River Dane**. Ignoring the footbridge, we continue (SW) on the riverside path, crossing a stile to reach the footbridge over **Black Brook**, where several paths converge (Wp.18 160M). On the far side, we bear right at two forks (note that the left hand path at the second fork goes to the rocky tor at Wp.7 near **Luds Church**) to follow the **Dane Valley Way**.

This deservedly popular path (very well used and rather churned up) runs along the hillside above the **River Dane**, almost an alpine mountain stream at this point. After passing through woodland for some distance, we emerge over a stile into meadowland and pass a farm, then cross more meadowland with thickets of gorse to approach another farm. Opposite, the foot of the **Wildboarclough Valley** is clearly visible, the **Dane** running through a short rocky gorge. Above the farm, our path briefly joins the farm track, following it downhill for a few yards before diverging left (Wp.19 190M) and descending into woodland, carpeted with bluebells in spring. The path continues through the woods until just before **Dane Bridge**, when it crosses a riverside meadow before briefly re-entering the woods to curve round to **Dane Bridge**.

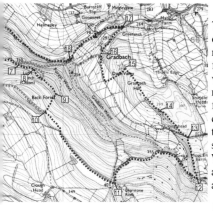

The considerable height and width of the Victorian bridge, built to replace an earlier one swept away in floods, is clearly visible from this viewpoint; that a bridge this large is necessary shows just how fierce the flash floods in this high rainfall catchment can be. The bridge marks the end of our walk (Wp.1 210M); a short step up the road to the west into **Wincle** offers refreshments as well as the chance to admire the pub sign, at **The Ship Inn**.

29 STAFFORDSHIRE GRIT: The Roaches & Ramshaw Rocks

Some of the Peak District's finest gritstone country is found in Staffordshire. It has its own distinctive character; while the gritstone strata between **Sheffield** and the **Derwent Valley** are mostly flat and form almost level 'edges', those on the Staffordshire side are folded into ridges or troughs, making for a much sharper profile where they are eroded. The country's most dramatic examples of this geology are found north of **Leek** and its reservoir at **Tittesworth** where a great trough or 'Syncline' of gritstone has been eroded on its sides, its western rim forming the rocky escarpments of **The Roaches**, its eastern rim by **Ramshaw Rocks** and its southern end by the great tilted slab of **Hen Cloud**. The centre of the trough is filled with younger 'Coal Measures' rocks; coal was mined in the **Goldsitch Moss** basin using primitive bell-pit techniques from the 17th to early 20th centuries.

We depart from the standard walk described in other guides with our route which provides a better appreciation of the geological landform, taking in **Hen Cloud** and **Ramshaw Rocks** as well **The Roaches**. We follow the trough's rim anticlockwise, starting with the airy viewpoint of **Hen Cloud** before ascending **Ramshaw Rocks** ridge, passing the eerie **Winking Man** rock, then along the gritstone outcrop through the nature reserve of **Gib Tor** before crossing **Goldsitch Moss** and the shoulder of **Gradbach Hill**. Saving the best until last, we return from **Roach End** along the crest of **The Roaches**, our south-easterly direction providing a much better route than the traditional north-westerly traverse. The walk can be extended by combining it with part of Walk 28, to take in **Luds Church** chasm.

The Roaches escarpment is a good place to see rock climbers tackling these popular crags. In the 1950s two Mancunian plumbers, Joe Brown and Don Whillans, were responsible for popularising this activity, honing their skills on these rocks. The house at the foot of the crags, used as a climbers' hut, is now named in commemoration of Don Whillans.

The region's popularity brings its own problems; car parking near **Roaches Gate** attracts car crime. An excellent and under-used alternative, (restricted to summer Sundays and bank holidays), is the Park and Ride service between **Tittesworth Reservoir** and **Roaches Gate**.

Safety Advice: 1. Take care near tops of crags. 2. Keep clear of ropes and belays in use by rock climbers

Access by bus: N°X18 (**Stoke** to **Sheffield** via **Leek** and **Buxton**, 2 hourly, 7 days). Ask the driver if he'll let you off at **Upper Hulme**, if not, alight at **Blackshaw Moor**, walk alongside the A53 to **Upper Hulme** then take the lane to **Roaches Gate**. N°221 (Summer Sundays/Bank Holidays only) Park and Ride service from **Tittesworth Reservoir**, some journeys also serve **Leek**.

Access by car: Take the A53 to **Upper Hulme**, then the lane to **Roaches Gate**. There's limited parking and the risk of car crime. For Park and Ride, (recommended) take the A53 to **Blackshaw Moor**, then the lane to **Tittesworth Reservoir**; park at **Severn Trent Water Visitor Centre**.

We start at the main gate leading on to **The Roaches**, by the bus stop on the lane from **Upper Hulme** (Wp.1). Heading up the track (E), we ignore the paths leading off to the left and continue until we reach a crossing of paths by gate in a wall on our right (Wp.2 4M). Turning right, we pass through a field and another gate, ascending on the path up **Hen Cloud**, enjoying views back towards **The Roaches**, across **Tittesworth Reservoir** and Staffordshire to the south and over to **Ramshaw Rocks**. Just before the top, a ruined wall heads off north-east; we'll follow it later. From the high ground the shape of the gritstone trough is clearly revealed, **The Roaches** and **Ramshaw Rocks** forming its western and eastern edges.

From the top of **Hen Cloud** (Wp.3 20M) we follow a faint path for a short distance until it starts descending, then take a course (NE) directly towards **Ramshaw Rocks**, deviating left to avoid the steep slope, to reach the ruined wall. After following it downhill, a faint path takes us into the woods on the right, parallel to the wall. We cross a faint path, then meet a second path and bear left to head (NW) across rough tussocky grassland. This path leads to a stile near the farm below, though it's easy to miss if you're too high on the hillside.

At the stile (Wp.4 35M), we cross the field and turn right after the next stile to follow the farm track down the valley alongside a wooded area of Scots pines. Where the track veers right (Wp.5 40M), we continue straight ahead, following a green track as it curves left by a barn, crosses a stile and a stream and rises to join another green track. We bear left and pass a house, the farm buildings of **Ferny Knowl** on our left. Now heading north on a tarmac lane, we follow it as it turns right and climbs east up a shoulder. Before the second bend to the right, a small wooden post on the left with a 'Fire Danger' sign signals the start of our faint path ascending steeply into the heather (Wp.6 45M) passing left of some rocks to meet and cross a lane (Wp.7 55M).

The Winking Man

We head onto the ridge of **Ramshaw Rocks**; there are several alternative paths on both sides of the rocks, well-used by rock climbers. After ascending steeply past rock formations to a grassy col between two sets of rocks, we descend (E) to a patch of red soil by **Winking Man** rock which overhangs the slope above the A53 road (Wp.8 75M). Dominating the view from the A53 road below, it looks like a cross between Pinocchio and Frankenstein, maniacally grinning, with a hole in the rock for an eye. If it winks at you, the legend goes, you're done for.

Returning to the ridge we ascend to the summit (Wp.9 80M), from where we take in views in all directions, then continue north along the ridge (ignoring the footpath sign pointing left), then join a sunken bridleway coming in from the left. When this bridleway curves right we turn left (Wp.10 95M), ignoring a stile in the fence on the right, to follow a footpath (NNW) descending gently towards a cottage below a group of rocks, first across heather moorland, then fields of rough grass and rushes.

The footpath sign pointing east

Crossing a stone slab bridge across a stream, we reach a lane (Wp.11 105M), cross it diagonally to the left, and take the path opposite past a cottage before heading north alongside a series of rocks, leading into **Black Brook Nature Reserve**. The path continues on the rocky ridge until a footpath sign, before a large group of rocks, points us east. The path crosses a wet area before turning north-east and crossing a stile into a clear felled area. The felling of conifers by Staffordshire Wildlife Trust in a habitat restoration plan was locally controversial; though alien to the landscape, many local residents valued the sheltered conifer wood.

As the path meets a lane opposite **Gib Torr** cottage (Wp.12 140M) we turn left to cross a brook and ascend a short rise, turning left at the top where a lane on the right joins; heading west, we continue along it past **Gib Tor** rocks on the left (a good picnic spot) and **Moss Top Farm** on the right, and descend into the flat land of **Goldsitch Moss** in the centre of the trough. After crossing another lane we join a road coming in from the left to reach a corner where the road turns sharp right and several tracks and paths meet (Wp.13 165M). To the south are a series of hummocks and hollows, the remains of **Goldsitch Moss** coal mines.

Ignoring the footpath and farm track, we take the rough track straight ahead, signposted 'Gradbach', and follow it west to the top of the rise.

Alternative Extension
(an additional one hour, 2½ miles/4 km)
At Wp.14 we meet the route of Walk 28 (see Walk 28, Wp.13) and can add **Luds Church** to the walk by following Walk 28 over **Gradbach Hill**, past **Gradbach Mill** to the **Black Brook** footbridge (Walk 28 Wp.18), taking the footpath signposted for 'Luds Church', then from Walk 28 Wp.7 to rejoin the main walk at **Roach End**.

Where it curves right, we turn left at a new gate in the wall leading onto access land (Wp.14 170M). Our route heads south along the crest of a ridge, overlooking **Black Brook Valley** on our right, dropping down to a bridleway at the end of the ridge, running alongside a wall (Wp.15 180M). We turn right, descending to the brook and crossing it on a footbridge.

From here the bridleway ascends steadily around a flank of **The Roaches**, passing a farm on the right, and becoming a partly surfaced track, to reach the lane and a junction of several paths at **Roach End** (Wp.16 210M). We turn left onto the heavily-used path ascending the ridge (SE) to **Roaches Top**. The path is heavily used, so steep sections have been paved to stop erosion. The rock scenery to the right, with more distant yet dramatic views over **Dane Valley** towards **Mow Cop** with many distinctively shaped rocks. From the **Roaches Top** trig point (Wp.17 225M) our path runs due south for a while before reaching the crest of the main escarpment. The main path runs a short distance to the east of the rim, but other paths allow us to walk along the rim to appreciate the dramatic views.

We come to **Doxey Pool** (Wp.18 235M), said to be bottomless and inhabited by a mermaid who entices travellers to a watery grave. From here the path along the rim is at its most dramatic, cliffs dropping sheer into woodland on the terrace below, challenging the rock climbers. The path descends to a dip (Wp.19 240M) where we leave the ridge on a path dropping steeply to the right, turning left below the crags, and continuing along their base, offering more views.

Doxey Pool

Rock climbers on the sheer cliffs

Turning right again (Wp.20 245M) we descend steps leading to the gate of **Rock House**, the Don Whillans memorial hut; note the 'Hobbit House' built into the rock, to the right of the house. Bearing right onto the open moor side, we follow the well-trodden path down to **Roaches Gate** just below Wp.1 - the end of our walk. Refreshments can be had at **The Roaches Tea Room** by the lane below **Hen Cloud**, **The Rock Inn** in **Upper Hulme**, **The Three Horseshoes** on the A53 at **Blackshaw Moor** or **The Lazy Trout** at **Meerbrook**, west of **Tittesworth Reservoir**.

30 BANDIT COUNTRY:
Forgers, Fugitives & Fighters of Flash

Three counties - Derbyshire, Staffordshire, Cheshire - meet in the lonely moors between **Leek** and **Buxton** in the upper reaches of the **Dane Valley** at **Three Shire Heads**. Several packhorse trails converged at their meeting point, but it was not only packhorses that passed through these borderlands. All kinds of lawless elements took advantage of the opportunity to evade justice by slipping across the county boundaries ahead of the law. Fugitives took refuge on these moors; illegal prize fights took place at **Three Shire Heads**, and although scant evidence remains to convince modern historians, **Flash** is reputed to have been a centre of the forger's trade, hence the expression 'Flash Money'. It was bandit country.

For walkers too, this was bandit country - given over to grouse, with public access limited to a few old packhorse trails and miners' and quarrymen's tracks - until September 19th 2004, when it was opened up by the 'Right to Roam' Countryside and Rights of Way Act. This walk takes full advantage of the new access rights, opening up a new circuit which deserves to become a classic Peak District moorland walk, taking in the uppermost reaches of the **River Dane**, and the gritstone heights of **Axe Edge**.

There's more than wild moorland to experience on this walk. The heights of **Axe Edge** offer incomparable views, and the scant remains of the once important industries of gritstone quarrying and coal mining (to fuel limekilns at **Harpur Hill** and **Buxton**) are revealed. We pass through the scattered smallholdings and family farmsteads of **Knotbury** and **Quarnford** - these farms never provided an easy living, and were often tenable only with supplementary income from mining and quarrying, a way of life that will probably be gone within a generation, leaving both rural social fabric and landscape the poorer.

Safety Advice: 1. Do not attempt in hill fog. 2. Keep clear of old coal mine workings.

N.B. Dogs are not allowed on the Right to Roam section across the grouse moors between **Danebower Quarries** and **Axe Edge End**, but there is an alternative route on the **Dane Valley Way** along public footpaths and lanes. The moor will be closed on shooting days in late summer/early autumn.

Access by bus: N°X18 (**Stoke** to **Sheffield** via **Leek** and **Buxton**, 2 hourly, 7 days) to **The Traveller's Rest**, **Flash Bar**, **Quarnford**. Walk NW alongside the A53, then left along the lane by **New Lodge Farm** to start walk at Wp.19.

Access by car: Take the A53, then go south-west on the lane to **Flash** (sharp turn from south). There's limited car parking on the lane opposite the village school on the east side of the village.

We start opposite the primary school in **Flash** (Wp.1), the highest school in England and the smallest in Staffordshire. Heading into the village (SW), we fork right by the church and pass **The New Inn** left, and an imposing former Wesleyan chapel right. Our lane descends steeply as it leaves the village, and we ignore footpath signs right and left, taking a farm track right (signed as a bridleway) at a right hand bend (Wp.2 13M). We descend to the farm (look out for South American Alpaca in the fields), fork left through a gate and bear left down a path to cross a ford beside a footbridge (Wp.3 22M). Ascending the steep bank left of the footpath sign (watch out for off road motorbikes), we then head west through a farm gate towards the smallholding of **Wicken Walls**. Just before reaching the buildings we cross a stile on our right (Wp.4 25M) and ascend alongside a fence to meet a rough tarmac lane (Wp.5 28M).

The abandoned smallholding

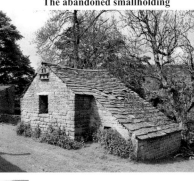

Turning left, we head past the smallholding of **Cockett Knowl** where the tarmac ends. Ignoring a footpath sign left and a track right, we continue on the track between walls until it widens and we reach a gateway on the left with an old squeeze stile and an OS bench mark carved into one of its uprights (Wp.6 40M). We fork left here to follow an old track (NW) down the hill past an abandoned smallholding on the left with a stone flag-roofed barn and dovecote.

Three Shire Heads

At the bottom of the hill we turn right, then right again by a bridge (Wp.7 45M) to follow a path signed for 'Three Shire Heads' which rises on a bluff above the **River Dane** to meet a track coming in from the right at a gate. Through the gate, the packhorse bridge at **Three Shire Heads** comes into view.

Closer, it's clear that here are in fact two bridges over separate streams which join by **Panniers Pool**, so named as it was used by packhorse men to water their beasts. Each stream forms a county boundary; we cross from Staffordshire to Derbyshire at the first bridge, then into Cheshire at the second bridge (Wp.8 65M). Its lawless past long gone, **Three Shire Heads** is now a peaceful place, and a good picnic spot.

Continuing on the path, we head north into Cheshire, the **River Dane** on our right, going over a stile on the right with a 'DVW' (**Dane Valley Way**) arrow after crossing a small *clough*. Following the signposted path, we continue through several stiles and a marshy section alongside the river and through a stretch where the valley narrows, to come to a series of old buildings - the **Danebower Colliery** yard. Last worked in the late 1800s, the arched roof of the main drift is on our right, but do not enter due to risks from cave ins and

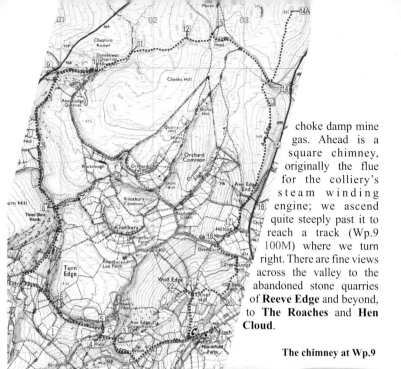

choke damp mine gas. Ahead is a square chimney, originally the flue for the colliery's steam winding engine; we ascend quite steeply past it to reach a track (Wp.9 100M) where we turn right. There are fine views across the valley to the abandoned stone quarries of **Reeve Edge** and beyond, to **The Roaches** and **Hen Cloud**.

The chimney at Wp.9

The track takes us east into the old quarry workings of **Danebower Quarries** (now re-colonised by nature) to end on a spoil heap with a steep, rocky descent down its side to a footpath sign pointing right (Wp.10 110M the route for those with dogs). Leaving the signed footpath, we take the faint path straight ahead running parallel with the river, now a small stream. The faint path, really more a sheep track, keeps to the grassy strip between the heather moor and the reeds in the valley bottom, slightly above the river.

After passing a *clough* on the opposite side we drop down to a confluence of streams (Wp.11 120M), fording the left hand one, **Tinkerspit Gutter** (coming back into Derbyshire). We ascend the bank between the two streams, taking care not to ascend too far into the heather, as the path runs east along the edge of the heather above the **River Dane**. The path turns left and we meet a ditch, then descend to the riverside, where we cross another small stream coming in from the right by hopping across clumps of reeds (Wp.12 130M). There's no path to follow, but two footpath signs can be seen ahead on the horizon, and you may spot the occasional vehicle on **Coalpit Lane** ahead. We head east towards these signs, picking the best route across the tussocks and heather, reaching a green track, where we turn left to the first footpath sign (Wp.13 140M). Turning right on **Coalpit Lane**, we head south-east, ignoring footpath signs and tracks left and right as we pass evidence of the coal mining that named this lane. The temptation to take short cuts across the moorland here should be resisted due to old mine workings. We pass a sign for a left hand bend, but before we come to the chevron signs, a faint unsigned path leaves the lane on the left by a small passing place (Wp.14 150M). From here, we'll be descending into **Cisterns Clough** on our right, but the path on the left is an optional additional there-and-back section leading to the trig point on the unnamed hill to the NNE (Wp.14A) with views over **Buxton** and **Harpur Hill**, before returning to Wp.14 (an additional 30 mins, 1.1 mile/1.8 km)

From Wp.14 we descend directly south into **Cisterns Clough**, crossing a track and the brook, then ascending to a faint path (formerly a tramway from the coal mines to the **Axe Edge** road), where we turn right for a short distance to avoid wet ground before turning left and heading south up the hillside. A line of grouse butts comes into view, and we head for the one on the left, with a number 8 on its wooden frame. We take a faint path uphill onto **Axe Edge** ridge, slightly east of the ridge's crest, to the summit (Wp.15 165M). The views are extensive in all directions, particularly to the east, where we can see right across the **White Peak** limestone country, as far as the gritstone edges above **Chatsworth**, and appreciate the scale of erosion that took place over millions of years to remove the gritstone cover from the centre of the Peak District. Many of the walks in this book are visible from this vantage point.

After absorbing the views, we continue along the ridge until it drops down to a track by cottages at **Axe Edge End** (Wp.16 175M). We take the track (SW) through the gate opposite, passing a terrace of cottages and dropping to a junction of lanes (Wp.17 180M) where we bear right to meet another junction by **Oxensitch Farm** (Wp.18 185M). Turning left, we ascend the lane as far as a stile on the right with a footpath sign (Wp.19 195M). Continuing ahead would bring us out on the A53 close to **The Traveller's Rest Inn** at **Flash Bar** (named after an old turnpike toll house, not the pub).

We turn right and head south on the footpath, crossing another stile. Where a marker post points the footpath ahead, we fork right and take a faint footpath uphill, with views across to **Flash Bar** and back towards **Axe Edge**. We meet a wall with an electric fence at the top, just before two TV aerials (Wp.20 205M), and follow it right, crossing it at a suitable point, (using spare clothing for insulation) and descend - still on access land - due west to a rusty gate below, to rejoin the public footpath (Wp.21 210M).

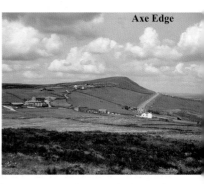

Axe Edge

A short detour through the gate, then a left fork, brings us to the viewpoint of **Wolf Edge** (Wp.22 215M) with **Dane Valley** spread out below us, another good picnic spot. Retracing our steps to the rusty gate we bear right, follow the track south, then fork left over the shoulder of the hill towards and past the last house in **Flash** village. We turn left across a stile by a gate, then left again onto the lane, to return into **Flash**, with refreshments at **The New Inn** before finishing by the village school (Wp.1 225M).

31 SHUTLINGSLOE: Macclesfield's Matterhorn

The distinctive pointed summit of **Shutlingsloe** is easily recognisable as one of the few peaks in the Peak - but its popular nickname, the 'Matterhorn of Cheshire' is surely taking Northern irony a bit too far! Nevertheless, this gritstone hill overlooking **Macclesfield Forest** and **Wildboarclough Valley** is a popular destination for Cheshire walkers. It was not always thus; it took a long campaign before access was gained, in the shape of a single public footpath traversing the summit from the forest plantations south-east to **Wildboarclough Valley**. This was the only route to the top - until September 2004, when Right to Roam opened up the surrounding moorlands north to **Buxtors Hill** and south to **Piggford Moor**. Our walk takes full advantage of these new access rights, creating an entirely new traverse providing fine moorland walking, accompanied only by the calls of the curlew, lapwing and skylark. There are wide views over the Cheshire plain and the gritstone moors by **The Cat and Fiddle** and **Shining Tor** and, by contrast, some woodland walking, unusual in the southern Peak District.

The name 'Macclesfield Forest' refers to its history of deer hunting and is applied to the whole area between **Macclesfield** and **The Cat and Fiddle** pass, not merely the plantations surrounding the reservoirs east of **Langley**. It's noted for its profusion of pubs - too many to visit on a single walk even for dedicated pub-crawlers - most of which have so far survived the trend for speculative conversion to private houses. We start and end at **Leather's Smithy Inn**, east of **Langley** facing **Ridgegate Reservoir**, pass **Hanging Gate** on the way to **Oakenclough**, and go close to **The Crag Inn** and **The Stanley Arms** in **Wildboarclough**.

3 | 3¾H | 7.2 miles/11½km | 440m / 440m | 3

Safety Advice: Take care in hill fog or stormy weather.

N.B. The **Piggford Moor** section may be closed in May for bird nesting, and dogs are not allowed here at any time to avoid disturbing wild birds. Alternative routes to **Shutlingsloe**: (1) via **The Crag Inn**, (2) via Walk 32.

Alternative start/finish
The car park 2km east of **Trentabank Reservoir** (Wp.13)

Access by bus: N°14/16 **Macclesfield-Langley**, Mon-Sat, frequent (no service Sunday or bank holidays): from the end of the route walk east along the lane past **Bottoms Reservoir** to reach **Leather's Smithy Inn**.

Access by car: Head south-east from **Macclesfield**, through **Langley**. Park on the road south-west of **Leather's Smithy Inn** alongside **Ridgegate Reservoir**.

From **Leather's Smithy Inn** facing **Ridgegate Reservoir** (Wp.1), we take the well-made track opposite running south-west along a low earth dam. An unusual iron squeeze stile takes us to a junction of paths at the far corner; we take the left hand track through a wooded knoll, waymarked for 'Shutlingsloe'. On the far side of the knoll the track slopes down to another

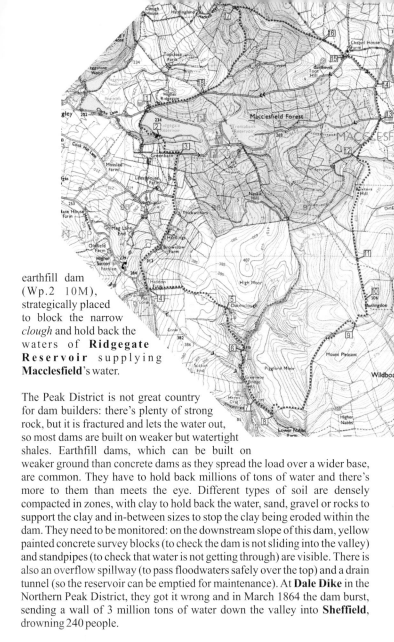

earthfill dam (Wp.2 10M), strategically placed to block the narrow *clough* and hold back the waters of **Ridgegate Reservoir** supplying **Macclesfield**'s water.

The Peak District is not great country for dam builders: there's plenty of strong rock, but it is fractured and lets the water out, so most dams are built on weaker but watertight shales. Earthfill dams, which can be built on weaker ground than concrete dams as they spread the load over a wider base, are common. They have to hold back millions of tons of water and there's more to them than meets the eye. Different types of soil are densely compacted in zones, with clay to hold back the water, sand, gravel or rocks to support the clay and in-between sizes to stop the clay being eroded within the dam. They need to be monitored: on the downstream slope of this dam, yellow painted concrete survey blocks (to check the dam is not sliding into the valley) and standpipes (to check that water is not getting through) are visible. There is also an overflow spillway (to pass floodwaters safely over the top) and a drain tunnel (so the reservoir can be emptied for maintenance). At **Dale Dike** in the Northern Peak District, they got it wrong and in March 1864 the dam burst, sending a wall of 3 million tons of water down the valley into **Sheffield**, drowning 240 people.

After crossing the dam crest, the path rises through the woods to the corner of a lane (Wp.3 15M) where we turn right (N.B. Dog walkers can continue ahead, then take concession bridleway for **Shutlingsloe** on right after 100 yards - see Walk 32). The narrow lane leads us south past several cottages, with views north-west across **Langley**, **Macclesfield** and (on a clear day) towards **Manchester Airport**. To the south-west is the distinctive knobbly outline of the **Sutton Common** tower, nicknamed by natives of Macclesfield as … er, let's not go there. As the lane joins a larger lane at a hairpin bend we take the upper fork to **The Hanging Gate** inn - a superb place to sit on the terrace at dusk on a summer evening and look out over the lights of **Manchester** (Wp.4 30M).

We take the public footpath on the left, opposite the pub, heading uphill (E) between two stone walls, crossing the stile at the top and following the path through a gateway right. Our route crosses an area of moorland, passing a pond on our right; apart from this path, this invitingly open area of moor is not open for access, being reserved for ground nesting birds, whose calls accompany us as we pass through. We drop towards the farm buildings of **Oakenclough**, bearing right on its track (Wp.5 55M) and passing left through a metal gate. Taking the path to the right of a small pond, we follow a small stream along the bottom of the attractive **Oaken Clough**.

At the foot of the *clough* (Wp.6 65M) the stream joins the larger **Highmoor Brook**. Although the moorland to the east of the brook is access land there is no means of crossing the wall, so we cross the stile by the footbridge and head south on the path following the brook, then bear left on the lane by **Greenway Bridge**. Our lane rises from the base of the valley and we take a track that forks left (Wp.7 70M) to continue south-west for around 300 metres to a gateway on the left (Wp.8). The gate is firmly fastened, but a stile leads on to the access land of **Piggford Moor**.

N.B. Dogs are not allowed here; for those with dogs, or if requiring refreshment, continue on the track, bearing right onto a footpath leading to **The Crag Inn** in **Wildboarclough**: then ascend **Shutlingsloe** by the public footpath from the SE.

From the stile we follow the track up the hillside, heading north then east, finally running alongside a wall and climbing to a corner. Here, we ignore the ladder stile and continue alongside the wall as it climbs onto a ridge, then makes a slight descent alongside **Sheep's Clough**, fine moorland walking, probably with only Lapwing, Curlew, Skylark and Snipe for company.

On top of Shutlingsloe

As we approach **Sheepsclough Gutter** stream our route leaves the wall, follows a duckboard crossing of marshy ground, and heads along a derelict wall almost directly towards the summit of **Shutlingsloe**. As the wall ends we meet a fence and follow it right to a gate (Wp.9 110M). The top of **Shutlingsloe** is north-east from here but there's another derelict wall and fence to cross; choose a good spot to negotiate this, then proceed uphill to the summit (Wp.10 120M). We are rewarded with views in all directions; note the viewpoint indicator, dedicated to Arthur Smith, who campaigned for access to this and other hills.

We leave the summit by the paved footpath heading north, initially descending steep steps alongside a wall.

At the second stile (Wp.11A 132M) our path crosses the wall on a stile and heads north-west across duckboards. Immediately after, we bear right, now keeping the wall on our right. After passing through a gap in a fence crossing our path, we head north along a flat moorland ridge to reach **Buxtors Hill**, with views across the forest to **Trentabank** and **Ridgegate** reservoirs and **Langley**. Descending (NNE), we pick up a faint track that leads us north-west through a gate (Wp.12 150M), then descend onto a forestry track to a junction of lanes close by a car park (Wp.13 158M). The lane opposite takes us north along a ridge to another junction of lanes (Wp.14 165M). Straight ahead would take us to **The Stanley Arms** for refreshment; we take the lane on the left, climbing north-west to run along a ridge with wide views before dropping to a small hamlet with a few farms and a chapel (Wp.15 170M).

The chapel at Wp.15

This simple chapel (built 1679, restored in 1884), far removed from ecclesiastical grandeur, perfectly fits its role of serving the scattered farmers and shepherds of these moors, and providing physical as well as spiritual shelter for travellers in inclement weather. A brief pause to look at its interior is worthwhile.

We leave the hamlet north-west on **Charity Lane**, ascending at first, then reaching the forest and a path diverging left through a wicket gate (Wp.16 180M). We take the path into the forest, passing quickly through conifers to mixed woodland. These forests were planted to keep grazing animals from polluting the gathering grounds of the reservoirs, so existing woodlands were left as they were.

Evidence of old stone walls and ruined buildings, relics of farmsteads abandoned when the reservoirs came, can be seen as we pass through. Our path descends to meet another path crossing at a signpost (Wp.17 200M); the moss-covered ruined barn (opposite) and the spring that once provided the farm's water are all that remains of the **Dimples Farm**.

We take the left fork signed 'Langley' and descend south, then south-west along a forestry track, with views of **Tegg's Nose** to our right. Meeting a lane (Wp.18 215M) we continue on the same heading, arriving at **Leather's Smithy Inn** (Wp.1 225M) - a splendid conclusion to a walk, supping an excellent pint of ale on the benches outside, looking out over **Ridgegate Reservoir**.

Leather's Smithy Inn

Roads that cross the high ground of the Peak and Pennines command particular respect from their users, and so are known by names, often dramatic and evocative, rather than mere numbers. No-one talks about the A537, A57 or A53; these are **The Cat**, **The Snake** and **Axe Edge**. Even the high junctions numbered 22, 23 and 24 on the M62 Motorway between Manchester and Leeds have become **Windyhill**, **Outlane Moor** and **Ainley Top**.

One of these great upland passes twists through high ground between **Macclesfield** and **Buxton**, passing the lonely **Cat and Fiddle Inn** from which it takes its name, at its summit nearly 1700 feet above sea level. It has the dubious honour of being the most dangerous road in Britain, mainly due to its popularity with bikers who come to take the slack out of it, and sometimes take a bit too much slack. Lumbering stone trucks from the quarries of **Buxton** add to the challenge; ten years of using **The Cat** as my commuter highway did nothing to lessen my respect for it.

For walkers, this high ground offers excellent moorland walking though, like the road, it commands respect. Although not particularly elevated, it seems to attract more than its share of weather. Having waited until May to research this route to avoid wintry weather, I still got caught wearing summer walking gear, in a storm of hail, snow and ice. Like centuries of travellers before me, I was grateful to take shelter and dry off in **The Cat and Fiddle Inn**.

The walk as described is long, though it's easy to split into two parts and use the N° 58 bus that runs along **The Cat** to complete the loop. Our walk description starts at **Teggs Nose Country Park** near **Macclesfield**, descends to **Langley** before traversing **Shutlingsloe** and descending again to the lonely **Wildboarclough Valley**, then climbs onto the moors to reach **The Cat and Fiddle Inn**. From here the N°58 bus can be used to return to **Walker Barn** (or direct to **Tegg's Nose** at weekends) or the return leg walked over **Shining Tor** and **Andrew's Edge**, descending to **Lamaload Reservoir**. A traverse of the moors returns us to **Tegg's Nose** via **Walker Barn**.

A word of warning; don't be tempted to make the return leg along the **The Cat** (A537). Its twisting nature and heavy goods traffic make it totally unsuitable for pedestrians. The unclassified road paralleling the A road to its south is a narrow rat-run used by local drivers (including this author), as a quicker alternative to the truck-bound A road, and is even worse - not for walkers.

| 5 | 6H | 13¾ miles/22km | | 815m / 815m | | 1 |

Safety Advice: 1. Severe weather in high moorlands is possible all year. 2. Great care is required if walking along or crossing the A537 or the parallel unclassified road, both of which carry heavy and fast traffic.

Alternative start/finish The Cat and Fiddle Inn, on A537, limited parking opposite the inn.

Access by bus: N°58 (**Macclesfield** to **Buxton**, 2 hourly, 7 days) to **Walker**

Barn (**Tegg's Nose** at weekends) and **The Cat and Fiddle Inn**.

Access by car: A537 to **Tegg's Nose** via the minor road from **Walker Barn**. Park at **Tegg's Nose Country Park**.

32A Tegg's Nose to Cat and Fiddle via Shutlingsloe
(3½ hours, 8.1 miles/13km)

Quarrying equipment at Wp.2

From the car park entrance at **Tegg's Nose** (Wp.1) we take the track (SW) with views over **Macclesfield** and the **Cheshire Plain**, then pass through a gate to continue on the surfaced path, soon bending sharp left into an area of old quarries, and leads to a collection of old quarrying equipment including a crane, a stone crusher and a rock saw (Wp.2 12M) complete with descriptive signboards. We then fork along a terrace (SW, notice ripple marks on some rocks), and shortly reach a track.

Opposite, we climb the steep path to the top of a heather-covered ridge (once quarry spoil mounds) and follow this south. The panorama is virtually 360 degrees, and takes in **Manchester**, with the **Lancashire Moors** beyond, the **Cheshire Plain**, **Mow Cop** in **Staffordshire**, **Macclesfield Forest**, **Shutlingsloe**, around to the solitary **Cat and Fiddle Inn** on the moors to the east, where we're heading. On a clear evening the view west extends over a hundred miles to **Snowdon** in North Wales - but far longer views, into the vastness of space, are had from the giant radio telescope at Jodrell Bank, a distinctive feature in the plain below, by the astronomers of the Lovell Observatory.

At the end of this ridge our path descends to meet another. We'll be going through the wooden squeeze stile to our right, but first we cross the path to reach the southernmost point of the high ground to enjoy views across the reservoirs of **Langley**. There's also signboard describing the local crafts and industries (Wp.3 20M). Returning to the stile, we pass through and start descending the gorse-covered hill, heading west towards a wall at first, then following the footpath as it curves south into a wooded area. At the foot of the hill we pass through a gate and cross the embankment of **Tegg's Nose Dam**, reaching a lane at its end (Wp.4 30M) which we cross diagonally left to take **The Gritstone Trail** across the dam of **Bottoms Reservoir**, curving left to join a lane opposite cottages. We bear left on the lane and follow it around the head of the lake, passing a waterworks on the right before turning right (Wp.5 40M) onto a track and following it past the waterworks. Across a cattle grid, we fork left to cross another cattle grid. Where the track starts climbing to the right (Wp.6 50M) we take a footpath left across a footbridge, then go up the opposite side of the valley through a wood rich with bluebells in spring.

At the top of the rise we turn right on a concession path signed for 'Shutlingsloe' to cross **Ridgegate Dam**, then climb a rise to meet a lane by an unusual metal squeeze stile (Wp.7 60M). We continue ahead (E) along the lane for a few yards, then turn right by a signboard onto a forest track, signed for 'Shutlingsloe', and ascend steadily for around a mile over the viewpoint of **Nessit Hill**.

Paved section climbing Shutlingsloe

The track descends for a while before merging with a path on the left from **Trentabank**, then ascends gently to another junction (Wp.8 95M) where we fork right for **Shutlingsloe**. Once through a gate and onto the moors, the path is paved with slabs to prevent erosion.

We continue ascending to a stile (Wp.9 105M) where we fork right to climb to the top of **Shutlingsloe** (Wp.10 120M) with its panoramic views across **C h e s h i r e** and **Staffordshire**.

We head south from the trig point along the summit crest, then bear left and head east down the steep slope towards a stile visible below at the edge of the moorland. Through the stile, we follow the marked path downhill which merges with a farm track to descend towards a belt of woodland.

On reaching the woodland (Wp.11 135M) we turn sharp left (the track ahead leads to **The Crag Inn**, and refreshments) and follow the track past **Banktop**, running alongside the edge of the woods (muddy in places), until it descends to the lane in the foot of the remote **Wildboarclough Valley** (Wp.12 146M). We take the footpath opposite across a footbridge and a meadow, then through the farmyard of **Clough House** where we bear right to reach a junction of lanes (Wp.13 150M).

Opposite, we take the track with a 'No vehicles' sign running alongside **Cumberland Brook**, which we cross on a new footbridge, the track then rising beside the wooded *clough* cut by the brook.

At the end of the trees we come on to the open moor. It's clear that this track was once a fairly substantial road, one of many built for packhorses superseded by the motor age. The brook has cut deeply into the dark shale at this point: this shale, although not often seen as it erodes easily, is actually more abundant than the hard gritstone in these measures, its weakness the cause of the landslides common in gritstone country.

Where this old road bends sharply to the right, crossing the brook by a waterfall, we come to a footpath sign (Wp.14 170M), bear left and follow a footpath up the *clough*, alternating from one side of the brook to the other until it zigzags out and onto the moor by two ruined walls.

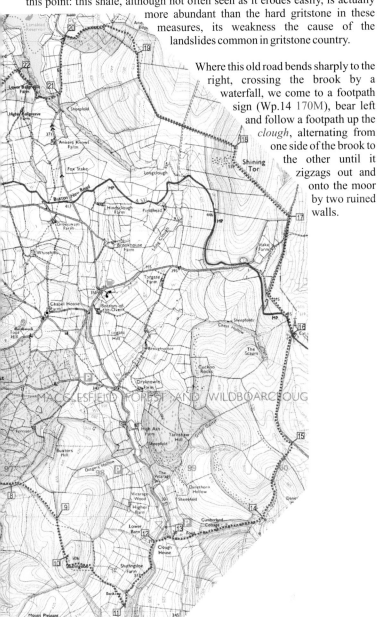

The path continues climbing alongside one of the walls until reaching the bridleway across **Danebower Moss** (Wp.15 190M) where we turn left and follow it north across the moors. **The Cat and Fiddle Inn** comes into sight as we pass through a gate and after crossing the main road carefully, we reach it (Wp.16 210M).

We head for the single storey extension on the right and find ourselves in the bikers' bar. Though unapologetically a bikers' pub, there's a lack of Heavy Metal or rowdy behaviour: these tend to be 'born-again' bikers of a certain age, happy to sip tea and discuss diesel spills before they get the motor runnin' and head out on the highway. Signs and leaflets around the bar provide an insight into the bikers' world; rather more sobering is the map outside of four years of motorbike accidents - many fatal - on the Cat.

If returning to **Tegg's Nose** on the N°58 bus, wait at the stop on the opposite (south) side of the road.. On weekdays, ask to be set down at **Walker Barn**, and follow the last stage of Walk 32B to get back to **Tegg's Nose**.

32B Cat and Fiddle to Tegg's Nose via Shining Tor
(2½ hours, 5.6 miles/ 9km)

If doing this section as a linear, bus out, walk back route, catch the N°58 bus from **Tegg's Nose** (at weekends) or **Walker Barn** (weekdays; walk from **Tegg's Nose** to **Walker Barn**) to **The Cat and Fiddle Inn**.

The Cat and Fiddle Inn

We start from **The Cat and Fiddle Inn** (Wp.16 0M). Keeping to the same side of the road as the inn, we carefully head north-west alongside the **Cat** to the first corner, where we take the track diverging right, to the crest of a ridge, looking down on the Cat road on the left and the moors of **Goyts Moss** on the right.

Through a gate, we ignore the footpath right to reach a junction of paths (Wp.17 20M) and turn left signed to 'Shining Tor', following the path (NW) across a long dip of peaty ground, the footpath repaired using geofabric and geogrid materials, more common in road building.

The path rises to a corner in the wall and we reach the trig point of **Shining Tor** on the opposite side of the wall, with views to **Shutlingsloe** and the Cheshire Plain. Remaining to the east of the wall, we continue for a few yards (a particularly squelchy section) to another paths junction (Wp.18 35M) where we turn left, signed to 'Lamaload Reservoir', on a path that runs across flat and fairly marshy ground to **Andrews Edge** ridge.

The view north-east towards **Cats Tor** is typical of gritstone country - a series of ridges formed by the harder gritstones, with lower ground between eroded into the softer shales.

The wall turns left at the end of the ridge (Wp.19 55M) and the path descends (NW) towards **Lamaload Reservoir**, heading to the right of a wooded area. As it leaves the moors the path runs west along a *clough* to the right of a stream, descending to meet a lane (Wp.20 80M) where we turn left. After climbing for a while the lane levels off with the reservoir on our right - look out for red deer and geese in the fields.

As we reach a wooded area on the right we turn right at a stile (Wp.21 95M) on a concession path descending into the woods, before climbing up to meet a track on the other side of the woods. Turning right on this track, we follow it across a stream, past an old barn (**Lower Ballgreave Farm**) and continue to the top of a rise crest, where a post with yellow arrows marks a junction of paths (Wp.22 105M). Our way is somewhat unclear here: we turn 90 degrees left and head south-west up the ridge to reach a gate in a wall ahead of us (Wp.23 110M). Through the gate, we continue (SW) to find ourselves running alongside a wall , then across a new footbridge and over a stile, and across a track until we reach a signposted fork in the footpath by an old piece of farm machinery (Wp.24 125M). We fork left, following the path as it twists through a *clough*, then continue (SW) to emerge on the side of the main road beside the millstone marking the National Park boundary (Wp.25 140M).

We cross the road, then bear right and follow it downhill into **Walker Barn** - take extreme care because of the traffic. Ignoring the first lane on the left, we take the second left turning opposite a house, formerly **The Setter Dog** pub. This road is one of the rat-runs, so continue very carefully, and making sure you're visible to motorists. We follow it uphill past a Methodist chapel to a crest, taking advantage of a short length of pavement on the right. Over the crest, we descend past **Windyway House** and find ourselves back at **Tegg's Nose** car park and the end of our walk (Wp.1 150M), a short drive from **Macclesfield** and refreshments.

WAYPOINT LISTS

(See notes on GPS on P.19)

1 THE MINES OF ECTON

Wp	Zn	Easting	Northing
1	SK	10269	59299
2	SK	10049	58808
3	SK	10097	58915
4	SK	10083	58712
5	SK	09881	58679
6	SK	10430	58088
7	SK	10319	58036
8	SK	10268	57787
9	SK	10255	57563
10	SK	09981	58001
11	SK	10050	58084
12	SK	09915	58350
13	SK	09846	58203
14	SK	09769	58127
15	SK	09575	58383
16	SK	09571	58075
17	SK	09203	57837
18	SK	09119	57824
19	SK	09534	58420
20	SK	09255	58698
21	SK	09671	58792

2 WETTON & NARROWALE HILLS

Wp	Zn	Easting	Northing
1	SK	10966	55361
2	SK	10906	55142
3	SK	10679	55273
4	SK	09930	54936
5	SK	09846	54930
6	SK	09864	54969
7	SK	10010	55140
8	SK	09843	55112
9	SK	09837	55686
10	SK	09758	56143
11	SK	09575	56112
12	SK	10068	56061
13	SK	10495	56259
14	SK	10709	56207
15	SK	11295	56602
16	SK	11710	57038
17	SK	12342	57249
18	SK	12566	56634
19	SK	12680	56696
20	SK	12633	56400
21	SK	12758	56040
22	SK	12379	55539
23	SK	11927	55471
24	SK	11126	55550
25	SK	10966	55361
10A	SK	10468	56648
15A	SK	10716	55841
21A	SK	13116	55583
21B	SK	12927	5 5809

3
WETTON HILL, SUGAR LOAF & ECTON HILL

Wp	Zn	Easting	Northing
1	SK	10963	55372
2	SK	10715	55744
3	SK	10707	56204
4	SK	10492	56259
5	SK	10126	56511
6	SK	09881	56499
7	SK	09790	56724
8	SK	10090	57339
9	SK	09605	57629
10	SK	09980	58003
11	SK	09908	58365
12	SK	09698	58305
13	SK	09534	58415
14	SK	09109	57756
15	SK	09215	57832
16	SK	09523	56120
17	SK	09750	56137
18	SK	09852	55707
19	SK	10699	56198
20	SK	10886	55463
21	SK	10959	55388

4
THE HIDDEN DALE

Wp	Zn	Easting	Northing
1	SK	10963	55371
2	SK	10912	55157
3	SK	10848	55039
4	SK	11170	54410
5	SK	11843	53594
6	SK	11934	53308
7	SK	11756	53052
8	SK	11637	53388
9	SK	12040	53293
10	SK	12267	52456
11	SK	12389	51526
12	SK	11104	52465
13	SK	10989	52581
14	SK	10616	53013
15	SK	10518	53988
16	SK	09991	54163
17	SK	10396	54285
18	SK	10963	55371
5A	SK	12030	53841

5
THE GATEWAY TO DOVEDALE

Wp	Zn	Easting	Northing
1	SK	16302	50479
2	SK	15892	50533
3	SK	15917	50631
4	SK	15382	50861
5	SK	15143	51042
6	SK	14735	51054
7	SK	14187	51254
8	SK	13813	51238
9	SK	13541	50850
10	SK	12809	51027
11	SK	12387	51530
12	SK	12838	51745
13	SK	12820	50616
14	SK	13261	50575
15	SK	14793	49732
16	SK	15569	50202
17	SK	16304	50479

6
MANIFOLD VALLEY LINEAR

Waypoints as for Walk 5 Wp.1-11, Walk 4 Wp.11-1, Walk 2 Wp.1-11, Walk 3 Wp.16-Wp13

7
REVIDGE, & THE HIDDEN PATHS OF WARSLOW

Wp	Zn	Easting	Northing
1	SK	08583	58768
.2	SK	08338	59323
3	SK	08306	59679
4	SK	08132	59888
.5	SK	07993	60272
.6	SK	07885	60042
.7	SK	07738	59915
.8	SK	07141	59605
9	SK	06769	59655
10	SK	06229	59679
11	SK	05827	59206
12	SK	06241	59089
13	SK	06520	59238
14	SK	06867	59024
15	SK	07384	59081
16	SK	08138	58904
17	SK	08198	58809
18	SK	08583	58768

8
DOVEDALE'S WESTERN RIM

Wp	Zn	Easting	Northing
1	SK	16376	50485
2	SK	15900	50537
3	SK	15915	50636
4	SK	15380	50861
5	SK	15134	51057
6	SK	15123	51360
7	SK	14699	51308
8	SK	14282	51548
9	SK	13981	51539
10	SK	13943	51896
11	SK	13958	52260
12	SK	14118	52646
13	SK	13921	53155
14	SK	13348	53475
15	SK	13125	53965
16	SK	12858	54214
17	SK	12877	54943
18	SK	13146	55561
19	SK	13423	55298
20	SK	13914	54707
21	SK	14290	53610
22	SK	14172	53148
23	SK	14522	51810
24	SK	15153	51397
25	SK	15613	50686
26	SK	16380	50487

9
DOVEDALE'S EASTERN RIM & THE WELLS OF TISSINGTON

Wp	Zn	Easting	Northing
1	SK	16361	50482
.2	SK	15901	50531
3	SK	15920	50637
4	SK	15593	50737
5	SK	15145	51404
6	SK	14737	51822
7	SK	14979	51922
8	SK	14600	52642
9	SK	14512	52891
10	SK	14363	53185
11	SK	14756	53745
12	SK	14519	53819
13	SK	14422	54125
14	SK	14002	54661
15	SK	13909	54706
16	SK	14637	55006
17	SK	14895	54781
18	SK	15773	54447
19	SK	17519	53558
20	SK	17433	52482
21	SK	17806	52262
22	SK	17572	52210
23	SK	16614	50348
24	SK	16364	50479

10
THE OTHER DOVEDALE

Wp	Zn	Easting	Northing
1	SK	12833	60436
2	SK	12830	58622
3	SK	13051	58496
4	SK	13318	58411
5	SK	13767	58009
6	SK	13706	58326
7	SK	13131	58409
8	SK	14214	56965
.9	SK	14352	56896
10	SK	14600	56138
11	SK	14614	55079
12	SK	14902	54778
13	SK	14631	54991
14	SK	13913	54709
15	SK	13146	55560
16	SK	13496	55683
17	SK	14394	56224

18	SK	14129	56666
19	SK	14207	56814
20	SK	14154	56882
21	SK	14352	56896
22	SK	14214	56965
23	SK	14541	58763
24	SK	14383	58923
25	SK	12829	60435

11
DOVEDALE LINEAR

Waypoints as for Walk 8 Wp.1-18, Walk 10 Wp.15-1 or 15-25

12
MINNINGLOW - 2000 YEARS OF HISTORY

Wp	Zn	Easting	Northing
1	SK	19464	58152
2	SK	20508	57632
3	SK	20511	57206
4	SK	20810	56974
5	SK	20342	56698
6	SK	20196	56432
7	SK	20463	56289
8	SK	20184	56234
9	SK	20048	56595
10	SK	20005	56925
11	SK	19803	57648
12	SK	20154	57523
13	SK	20520	57256
BUS	SK	19202	59116

13
MOYNASH, ARBOR LOW & UPPER LATHKILL

Wp	Zn	Easting	Northing
1	SK	15001	66560
2	SK	15127	66529
3	SK	15107	66329
4	SK	15184	66228
5	SK	15886	65566
6	SK	16311	64949
7	SK	16383	64634
8	SK	16583	64421
9	SK	16767	64280
10	SK	16521	63948
11	SK	15892	63952
12	SK	15938	63566
13	SK	15819	63333
14	SK	16791	64284
15	SK	16833	64601
16	SK	17204	64896
17	SK	17239	65324
18	SK	17450	65514
19	SK	16184	66126
20	SK	15748	66452
16A	SK	16942	65247
19A	SK	16425	66112

14
STANTON MOOR: WITCHES, WARRIORS & QUARRIERS

Wp	Zn	Easting	Northing
1	SK	25646	65698
2	SK	25679	64499
3	SK	25571	64206
4	SK	25391	63725
5	SK	25325	63551
6	SK	25239	63777
7	SK	25090	63994
8	SK	25019	63541
9	SK	24909	63502
10	SK	25126	63397
11	SK	25204	63246
12	SK	24826	62733
13	SK	24548	62535
14	SK	24407	62251
15	SK	24092	62217
.16	SK	23659	62178
17	SK	24115	62461
18	SK	24186	62706
19	SK	24346	62785
20	SK	24606	63365
21	SK	24642	64149
22	SK	24580	64806
23	SK	24673	65325
24	SK	25405	65586

15
LIMESTONE & GRITSTONE FROM ELTON

Wp	Zn	Easting	Northing
1	SK	22170	60960
2	SK	21840	60934
3	SK	21135	61391
4	SK	20103	59690
5	SK	19051	60265
6	SK	18964	60493
7	SK	19597	61826
8	SK	20105	61685
.9	SK	20914	61617
10	SK	21004	61971
11	SK	21115	61948
12	SK	21341	61994
13	SK	21754	61437
14	SK	22075	62013
15	SK	22215	62005
16	SK	22416	62203
17	SK	22398	62285
18	SK	22506	62335
19	SK	22691	62368
20	SK	22747	62326
21	SK	22603	62267
22	SK	22841	61858
23	SK	22886	61361
15A	SK	22297	61910
15B	SK	22309	62647

16
LATHKILL & BRADFORD

Wp	Zn	Easting	Northing
1	SK	22026	64556
2	SK	21392	65115
3	SK	21162	65458
4	SK	21199	65643
5	SK	20280	66133
6	SK	19630	66144
7	SK	19400	65860
8	SK	18420	65756
9	SK	17458	65511
10	SK	16598	66055
11	SK	16180	66133
12	SK	16418	66129
13	SK	16423	66185
14	SK	16577	66097
15	SK	16417	66567
16	SK	17287	66317
17	SK	17634	66054
18	SK	17458	65511
19	SK	17267	65306
20	SK	18042	65049
21	SK	19266	64487
22	SK	19888	64187
23	SK	19710	63776
24	SK	19580	63188
25	SK	20108	63277
26	SK	19900	63337
27	SK	19956	63633
28	SK	20886	63997
29	SK	21346	64010

17
TADDINGTON & CHELMORTON

Wp	Zn	Easting	Northing
1	SK	14018	71104
2	SK	13916	71014
3	SK	12699	70682
4	SK	12091	70513
5	SK	11911	69691
6	SK	11456	70213
7	SK	11521	70311
8	SK	11370	70633
9	SK	12078	70564
11	SK	12375	71041
12	SK	12235	71705
13	SK	12803	72003
14	SK	13420	71650
15	SK	13711	71642
16	SK	13963	71941
17	SK	14233	71528
18	SK	14430	71522
19	SK	14421	71401
20	SK	14403	71061
21	SK	14438	70828

18

ROOKERY & MAGPIE

Wp	Zn	Easting	Northing
.1	SK	19416	69780
.2	SK	19085	69587
3	SK	19041	69649
4	SK	19100	69420
5	SK	18491	69722
6	SK	17922	69306
7	SK	17979	68859
8	SK	17272	68185
9	SK	17430	68071
10	SK	17304	68440
11	SK	17479	68781
12	SK	17363	69203
13	SK	16945	69948
14	SK	16751	70028
15	SK	16500	69995
16	SK	16916	70209
17	SK	16981	70104
18	SK	17931	69604
19	SK	19439	69593
20	SK	19658	69763
21	SK	19425	69789

19

LITTON, CRESSBROOK DALE, PETER'S STONE & ASHFORD

Wp	Zn	Easting	Northing
1	SK	16399	75142
2	SK	16577	75140
3	SK	16693	74956
4	SK	16799	74762
5	SK	17306	75435
6	SK	17631	75368
7	SK	17378	75258
8	SK	17148	73267
9	SK	17072	73063
10	SK	17348	72725
11	SK	18170	71881
12	SK	17645	71413
13	SK	18451	71538
14	SK	19450	70010
15	SK	19659	69763

20

FIN COP & HOB'S HOUSE

Wp	Zn	Easting	Northing
1	SK	18481	71560
2	SK	18213	71812
3	SK	17645	71413
4	SK	17516	71289
5	SK	17428	71143
6	SK	17432	70907
7	SK	17511	71222
8	SK	17795	71311
9	SK	18481	71562

21

WYEDALE

Wp	Zn	Easting	Northing
1	SK	18494	71490
2	SK	18446	71606
3	SK	17176	72524
4	SK	16835	72428
5	SK	15679	72685
6	SK	15485	72571
7	SK	15182	72442
8	SK	14008	72123
9	SK	13430	71643
10	SK	12799	71999
11	SK	12638	72295
12	SK	12303	72021
13	SK	11528	72586
14	SK	11627	72676
15	SK	11262	72644
16	SK	11933	72781
17	SK	12559	73078
18	SK	12315	73533
19	SK	12781	73465
20	SK	13320	73301
21	SK	13828	73247
22	SK	14018	73202
23	SK	15846	72977
24	SK	17252	72804
25	SK	17758	72144
26	SK	18496	71493

22

A LINEAR WALK ALONG WYEDALE

Waypoints as for Walk 21
Wp.15-26, Walk 19 Wp.13-15

23

LONGSTONE EDGE & HIGH RAKE

Wp	Zn	Easting	Northing
1	SK	19863	71845
2	SK	19676	72175
3	SK	18948	72832
4	SK	18648	73210
5	SK	18883	73299
6	SK	18979	73633
7	SK	19496	73575
8	SK	19736	73799
9	SK	20467	73228
10	SK	21795	73642
11	SK	22493	73947
12	SK	21817	73711
13	SK	21538	73075
14	SK	20585	73030
15	SK	20167	71986
16	SK	19863	71845

24

HADDON & CHATSWORTH

Wp	Zn	Easting	Northing
1	SK	25599	65855
2	SK	25524	65934
3	SK	25039	66804
4	SK	24415	66965
5	SK	22973	67016
6	SK	23122	66539
7	SK	22928	67549
8	SK	23014	67889
9	SK	22548	68704
10	SK	23431	68834
11	SK	24696	68716
12	SK	25127	70017
13	SK	25718	70184
14	SK	25850	68709
15	SK	25748	68200
16	SK	25599	65855

25

CHATSWORTH

Wp	Zn	Easting	Northing
1	SK	25815	72135
2	SK	25836	71850
3	SK	26486	71918
4	SK	26815	71998
5	SK	27679	72094
6	SK	28005	71883
7	SK	28435	71420
8	SK	28627	69244
9	SK	28738	69246
10	SK	28210	68755
11	SK	27997	68399
12	SK	28351	68382
13	SK	27125	69067
14	SK	26988	69258
15	SK	26731	69453
16	SK	26619	70070
17	SK	26721	70158
18	SK	26524	70617
19	SK	26558	70690
20	SK	26597	70945
.21	SK	26708	71269
22	SK	26988	71733
23	SK	25815	72135

26

THE DRAGON'S BACK

Wp	Zn	Easting	Northing
1	SK	08865	64942
2	SK	09026	65177
3	SK	09558	65951
4	SK	08954	66328
5	SK	08855	66648
6	SK	08742	66747
7	SK	09004	67013
8	SK	08624	67021
9	SK	08446	66833
10	SK	08118	66775
11	SK	08148	66880
12	SK	07961	66970
13	SK	07821	67009
14	SK	07673	67078

Wp	Zn	Easting	Northing
15	SK	07065	67347
16	SK	06729	67644
17	SK	06472	68200
18	SK	05840	68026
19	SK	05901	67579
20	SK	06191	66949
21	SK	06304	66869
22	SK	06371	66660
23	SK	06508	66534
24	SK	08100	65158
25	SK	08198	65173

27

BURTON TO LONGNOR

Wp	Zn	Easting	Northing
1	SK	05940	73718
2	SK	05803	73512
3	SK	05685	73497
4	SK	05446	72931
5	SK	05037	72518
6	SK	05406	71750
7	SK	05030	71891
8	SK	04361	71827
9	SK	04562	71165
10	SK	04723	70231
11	SK	04960	70135
12	SK	05234	69653
13	SK	05227	69095
14	SK	05582	69030
15	SK	05920	69268
16	SK	06298	68778
17	SK	06516	68314
18	SK	06477	68201
19	SK	06744	67645
20	SK	07063	67343
21	SK	07676	67086
22	SK	07832	66805
23	SK	08227	65947
24	SK	08604	65587
25	SK	08816	65003
26	SK	08874	64928

28

DANE BRIDGE, GRADBACH & LUDS CHURCH

Wp	Zn	Easting	Northing
1	SJ	96542	65190
2	SJ	96517	65066
3	SJ	96535	64835
4	SJ	97426	65284
5	SJ	97358	65394
6	SJ	97770	65557
7	SJ	98496	65758
8	SJ	98685	65698
9	SJ	98911	65422
10	SJ	98800	65242
11	SJ	99572	64492
12	SK	00491	64552
13	SK	00375	64985
14	SK	00068	65263

Wp	Zn	Easting	Northing
15	SJ	99678	65701
16	SJ	99402	65847
17	SJ	99630	66120
18	SJ	99045	65788
19	SJ	97079	66062
20	SJ	96541	65188

29

STAFFORDSHIRE GRIT

Wp	Zn	Easting	Northing
1	SK	00436	62111
2	SK	00705	62075
3	SK	00853	61576
4	SK	00999	61938
5	SK	01294	61692
6	SK	01616	61906
7	SK	01752	61949
8	SK	02022	62361
9	SK	02000	62456
10	SK	02070	62927
11	SK	01839	63562
12	SK	02172	64826
13	SK	00848	65056
14	SK	00379	64985
15	SK	00489	64549
16	SJ	99565	64497
17	SK	00106	63893
18	SK	00393	62861
19	SK	00557	62510
20	SK	00601	62250
21	SK	00437	62113

30

BANDIT COUNTRY

Wp	Zn	Easting	Northing
1	SK	02651	67254
2	SK	01830	66922
3	SK	01567	67179
4	SK	01432	67187
5	SK	01462	67283
6	SK	00849	67573
7	SK	00572	67766
8	SK	00937	68543
9	SK	00980	69950
10	SK	01392	69982
11	SK	01772	70161
12	SK	02369	70313
13	SK	02648	70371
14	SK	03273	69875
15	SK	03251	69285
16	SK	03079	68658
17	SK	02927	68305
18	SK	02721	68145
19	SK	02923	68033
20	SK	02739	67598
21	SK	02423	67638
22	SK	02281	67654
23	SK	02654	67255
14A	SK	03503	70622

31

SHUTLINGSLOE

Wp	Zn	Easting	Northing
1	SJ	95265	71544
2	SJ	95347	71274
3	SJ	95601	71072
4	SJ	95270	69658
5	SJ	96106	69464
6	SJ	96304	69009
7	SJ	96408	68515
8	SJ	96617	68338
9	SJ	97510	69312
10	SJ	97647	69578
11	SJ	97525	69982
12	SJ	97536	71050
13	SJ	97776	71449
14	SJ	97751	71813
15	SJ	97403	72082
16	SJ	97153	72269
17	SJ	96217	72614
18	SJ	95851	71708
19	SJ	95265	71544

32

THE CAT & FIDDLE MOORS

Wp	Zn	Easting	Northing
1	SJ	95028	73276
2	SJ	94826	72579
3	SJ	94776	72254
4	SJ	94587	71716
5	SJ	94901	71466
6	SJ	95193	71204
7	SJ	95602	71073
.8	SJ	97022	70356
.9	SJ	97532	69976
10	SJ	97649	69572
11	SJ	98255	69080
12	SJ	98606	69748
13	SJ	98798	69771
14	SJ	99784	69980
15	SK	00088	70771
16	SK	00123	71884
17	SK	00079	73149
18	SJ	99510	73885
19	SJ	98438	74857
.20	SJ	97626	75050
21	SJ	97583	74456
22	SJ	97115	74692
.23	SJ	96978	74581
24	SJ	96111	74004
25	SJ	95732	73793
26	SJ	95028	73276

adit   horizontal tunnel giving access to a mine

Barmote Laws   laws governing lead mining and mineral rights, within a *liberty*

Barmote Court   court with jurisdiction to adjudicate *Barmote Law* cases within a *liberty*

belland ground   land contaminated with lead dust or *belland*, likely to poison grazing livestock

chert   flint-like silica mineral, found as nodules or layers in limestone, ground to make hard glaze for pottery

clough   steep-sided valley or gully in gritstone country

gangue   non-metallic minerals found in veins with lead ore, such as fluorspar and calcite; once discarded, these minerals are now mined in their own right

grange   farmstead originally owned and operated by a pre-reformation monastic order

launder   channel to lead water to a mill or mine

liberty   mining district within the lead bearing area of the Peak District, governed by its *Barmote Laws*

rake   vertical vein containing minerals including lead and *gangue* minerals

scarp   steep slope cutting across rock layers where inclined rock strata are eroded

shack   place where stream or river disappears below ground in limestone country; also *shakehole*, *swallet*

sough   tunnel excavated horizontally from bottom of valley to drain groundwater from mining area

tor   residual masses of harder rock remaining in place, typically on top of hills, after erosion of softer rock surrounding

trommel   mesh screen formed into a cylinder that can be turned, allowing pieces of rock to be sorted

whim   horse-operated winding gear, originally found as headgear to lead mines before steam engines were introduced in the early to mid 1800s

APPENDICES

A Google search in August 2005 for "Peak District" revealed over 4 million internet records, so there's no shortage of information! A few are listed here. Tel Nºs are in red.

WALKING INFORMATION

www.bbc.co.uk/weather/ukweather/midlands www.visitpeakdistrict.com (weather forecasts; on high ground, always assume the worst case scenario!)

www.countrysideaccess.gov.uk/where_you_can_go.php (Right to Roam info, including temporary restrictions. Click on "Lower North West")

www.ramblers.org.uk (useful guide on walking and the law; use their online form to report footpath obstructions, etc.)

GENERAL/LOCAL INFORMATION

www.peakdistrict-npa.gov.uk (official Peak District National Park Authority (PDNPA) site, covers guided walks and the ranger service 01629 816200)

Ranger Service 01629 816290   rangers@peakdistrict.gov.uk

Ranger Service District Office, South (Millers Dale) 01298 871869 millersdale@peakdistrict.gov.uk

Info for **Buxton** area www.buxtononline.net

www.peaklandheritage.org.uk (**historical info** from Derbyshire County Council's excellent local studies library 01629 585579 in collaboration with PDNPA)

www.chatsworth-house.co.uk 01246 565300

www.haddonhall.co.uk 01629 812855

www.pdmhs.com (**Peak District Mines Historical Society**, c/o Mining Museum, Matlock Bath 01629 583834)

www.nationaltrust.org.uk/main/w-index.htm 0870 458 4000

Ilam Park 01335 350503 (Estate office) 01335 350245 (Visitor centre)

www.english-nature.org.uk 01733 455101, Peak District and Derbyshire office 01629 816640

www.cressbrook.co.uk (independent with local info)

TOURIST INFORMATION

www.visitpeakdistrict.com (accommodation, local information, what's on, weather)

Ashbourne, 13 Market Place DE6 1EU 01335 343666

ashbourneinfo@derbyshiredales.gov.uk
Bakewell, Old Market Hall, Bridge Street DE45 1DS 01629 813227
bakewell@peakdistrict-npa.gov.uk
Buxton, The Crescent SK17 6BQ 01298 25106 tourism@highpeak.gov.uk
Leek, 1 Market Place ST13 5HH 01538 483741
tourism.services@staffsmoorlands.gov.uk
Matlock Crown Square DE4 3AT 01629 583388 matlockinfo@derbyshiredales.gov.uk
Matlock Bath, The Pavilion DE4 3NR 01629 55082
matlockbathinfo@derbyshiredales.gov.uk

ACCOMMODATION -GENERAL

www.peakdistrict-nationalpark.com (linked to the Cressbrook.co.uk site)
www.derbyshire-thepeakdistrict.co.uk   www.peakdistrictonline.co.uk
Local Self Catering and **B&B**   www.peakdistrictbreaks.co.uk
Farm based self catering/B&B   www.peakdistrictfarmhols.co.uk

GETTING AROUND

www.nationalrail.co.uk   08457 48 49 50
www.midlandmainline.com (excellent Peak Explorer offer 08457 125 678)
www.derbysbus.net   058 456 058 058
www.countrygoer.org/peak.htm (public transport info)

THINGS TO BUY

www.peakdistrictproducts.co.uk   Locally produced arts, crafts and fine foods
www.peakdistrictfoods.co.uk   Local food producers including Chatsworth Farm Shop

BIBLIOGRAPHY

Peak Bouldering Allen Williams and Allen James (Rockfax.com, 1998 SBN 1-873341-45-8) The wacky world of "Bouldering" (low level climbing without ropes) notable for originality & frequent scatology, used to name natural landscape features.

Classic Caves of the Peak District Iain Barker (Crowood Press, 1997 ISBN 1-86126-058-X) Speleologist's guide for speleologists - not for casual visitors!

Rocks & Scenery of the Peak District Trevor D. Ford (Landmark Publishing Ltd, 2002 ISBN 1-84306-026-4) Classic geology guide resists the temptation to use jargon.

Lead Mining in the Peak District T. D. Ford and J. H. Rieuwerts (eds), (Peak District Mines Historical Society/Landmark Publishing, 2000 ISBN 1-901522-15-6) History and relics of this important industry.

The Copper and Lead Mines of the Manifold Valley, North Staffordshire Lindsey Porter and John Robey (Landmark Publishing Ltd 2000 ISBN 1-901522-77-6)

Peakland Roads and Trackways A.E. and E. M. Dodd (Landmark Publishing 2000 ISBN 1-84306-129-5) How people got around before railways and cars.

The Peak District: The Official National Park Guide Roly Smith (Photos by Ray Manley) (Pevensey Guides 2000 ISBN 1-898630-1-0) Excellent photography sums up the essence of this landscape, backed up by knowledgeable writing.

Hidden Derbyshire Richard Stone (Countryside Books 2001 ISBN 1-85306-715-6) Little known historical details and facts.

Arbor Low, A Guide to the Monuments John Barnatt and Ray Manley (Peak National Park 1996 ISBN 0-907543-74-X) Short guide sometimes available by the Honesty Box at Upper Oldhams Farm.

The 1932 Kinder Trespass Benny Rothman (Willow Publishing 1982 ISBN 0-9506043-7-2) Uncompromising personal view of the Kinder Scout mass trespass by its late instigator. Its historical relevance to walking throughout the Peak District merits its inclusion, although Kinder Scout is not covered by this book.

In the Highlands of Staffordshire W H Nithsdale (The Moorland Press 1906 Facsimile Reprint Churnet Valley Books) Edwardian guide; fascinating insight into tourism and the countryside a century ago.

Peak District Bus Timetable Derbyshire County Council, reprinted twice yearly. Available from bookshops, libraries and by post (order from www.derbysbus.net), essential information for bus users - 50p well spent.

Memories of the Moorland Farmer Susan Gaukroger and Joyce Halliday (eds) (History Live 1994) Transcripts of recollections of lifelong residents.

Alec Gilman's Wetton Pen Gilman (1997 ISBN 0-9532251-0-0) Autobiographical and detailed description of farming and village life in the Peak District.

The Hike, and the Art of One-Downmanship Don Shaw (Tideswell Press 2004 ISBN 0-9546878-0-9) - just about says it all!

INDEX OF PLACE NAMES

Walk! Wire-O Spiral Bound Guidebooks are designed to be used with:
- DWG's plastic slipcover (PSC), which prevents the binding from catching on pockets and increases durability -
- - and our clear plastic All Weather Book Bag (AWBB) with grip-top seal which allows the book to be folded back displaying 2 pages, then sealed, impervious to weather conditions.

To obtain your PSC and AWBB for this book, send a C5 (9 x 7 inch) SAE with 47p stamp, to:

(Code 9781904946119)
Discovery Walking Guides
10 Tennyson Close
Northampton NN5 7HJ